Red Corridor

Red Corridor

(Jharkhand Perspective)

By

Col. (Dr.) Rajesh Kumar

Jharkhand Raksha Shakti University

Ranchi

KALPAZ

First Published, 2022

Published by

Kalpaz Publications
C-30, Satyawati Nagar,
Delhi – 110052
E-mail: kalpaz@hotmail.com
Ph.: 9212142040

Printed at: G. Print Process, Delhi

Distribution Network
gyanbooks.com
India, USA, Canada, UK, Australia, France

Cataloging in Publication Data—DK
Courtesy: D.K. Agencies (P) Ltd. <docinfo@dkagencies.com>

Kumar, Rajesh, author.
Red corridor / Col. (Dr.) Rajesh Kumar.
pages cm
Includes bibliographical references.
ISBN 9789351283461 (HB)

1. Naxalite movement—India—Jharkhand. 2. Communism—India—Jharkhand. I. Title.

LCC HX395.J43K86 2018 | DDC 335.430954127 23

CONTENTS

Foreword

Naxal terror has become a threat to the security of India. With passage of time, the menace has been increasing. Jharkhand since its formation had been in clutches of naxalism; the insurgencies numbering to devastating consequences. This presents a critical, analytical picture of Naxalism, and has been concentrated to areas of Jharkhand. The state now stands at topmost position, the other states lag behind.

This book consists of nine chapters. The first chapter is an introduction. Chapter 2 traces the evolution of Maoism as an ideological concern internationally as well as its upsurge in India. The third chapter highlights the nature of incidences in the state of Jharkhand with yearly comparisons for analytical purpose. Data has also been presented in tabulated form. The following chapter is a historical overview of Jharkhand with mention of existing districts and tribal population. Study with such background has helped in clarifying situations for further intensive study. The fifth chapter traces evolution of Naxalism in Jharkhand particularly, with lights on district based uprisings as well. Chapter 6 puts light on the present day scenario of naxal consequences. Included among this are the naxal and corporate nexus and facts on levy extractions. Chapter 7 puts light on counter naxal strategies. Programs of such kind together with its limitations have been critically studied through this chapter. Following this is the 8th chapter which presents some case studies and further scenario that has arisen due to counter operations, government perspectives. The chapter unfolds the lacunae in state programs too. The last is the ninth chapter which consists of conclusive analysis. Solutions to the menace with an approach have also been included. At the end of the report, appendix with pictures concerning Maoism has been added.

Objectives

1. Trace the evolution of Maoism.
2. Understand and relate its spread in India.
3. Study the conditions in Jharkhand and relate causes for penetration of Naxalism in the state.
4. Search the supportive bases for Maoism.
5. Know the state's intensions towards Naxalism and its eradication.
6. Present a concluding analysis and suggest an approachable solution.

Methodology

Present study is empirical in nature. An analytical approach has been made with deductive methods. The figures mention in this book has been gathered from secondary sources, with a prior care for their authenticity.

Tools for comparative studies include tabulations. Conversations with journalists, government officials, officials from Non Governmental Organisations and local people in Ranchi have been help for critical understandings. Analytical reports on the subject have also been studied and instances from them have been mentioned by me in this report.

A lack of data gathered through field works can be mentioned among the limitations.

The study is outcome of cooperation, support, encouragement and assistance extended to me in several forms. I am grateful to-

Dr. S.P. Singh, Director,Human Rights Education, Ranchi University;

Dr. P.K. Singh, Co-ordinator, Human Rights, Ranchi University; Mr. Madhukar, Advisor Editor/Khabar Mantra, Ranchi;

IPS. (Retd.) B. K. Sinha, Guest Faculty, Human Rights, Ranchi University;

Mr. Vishal Kumar, Advocate (High Court, Ranchi);

Mr. Gopi Nath Ghosh, Social activist, (BIRSA, NGO)

The Thin Red Line Gets Thicker

The Naxal movement, already strong in many states, is expanding despite the "massive, coordinated operations" launched as counter-offensives

Chapter – I

Introduction

On 7th January 2013, headlines flashed a strange and inhumane incidence in Jharkhand led by Naxalites. A 1.5-kg improvised explosive device had been implanted inside the abdomen of a CRPF personnel killed in an encounter with Naxals in Jharkhand's Latehar district. Also two lEDs had been placed beneath the bodies of two jawans at the encounter site. In the first case, the bomb was recovered and in the second, the lEDs exploded leading to some casualties. "Had the bomb inside the body exploded before being detected by doctors at a local hospital, it would have claimed many innocent lives. It was a booby trap, a first of its kind, where the IED was meticulously concealed inside the stomach that had multiple stitches. The IED was a pressure bomb prototype which explodes on being disturbed. This is a first-of-its-kind incident where it is evident that Maoists are under tremendous pressure from security forces and thinking of new ways to target them," a senior official of the Ministry of Home Affairs (MHA) said. In a major setback to the government's offensive against Maoists in Latehar district, 10 security personnel, including nine from the CRPF lost their lives.

"The Naxalites, also sometimes called the Naxals, is a loose term used to define groups waging a violent struggle on behalf of landless labourers and tribal people against landlords and others. The. Naxalites say they are fighting oppression and exploitation to create a classless society. Their opponents say the Naxalites are terrorists oppressing people in the name of a class war."

Naxal movements have been the origins from communist movements the movements similar to those which were made popular throughout the world. The period after 2nd world war had two main powers, USSR and China with communist ideologies. A policy of neutrality adopted by India also provided it the strategic relations with Soviet Union and simultaneous growth of communist ideologies. The Maoism prevailing in India today has been a consequence of splits in the Communist Party of India (CPI) which had been influenced by increasing tensions due to Moscow's demand to moderate its relations of oppositions with Congress. The international communist movements saw splits resulting from Mao Zedong's opposition to Nikita Khrushchev's policies which according to him were pro western. The world further saw the USSR- China split and growth of Maoism as more radical form of Marxist-Leninist philosophies. The India-China border war of 1962, neo liberal policies of governments, were among the earlier reasons for split in CPI to form Communist Party of India (Marxist) and further splits.

Naxalism has become a devastative truth and a menace to the state of Jharkhand which now stands at the top of the list of states included in the "Red Corridor". The Naxalite movement came into being as a result of prevailing social and economic issues. The Naxalbari uprising of 1967 was one in which the tribals had taken up arms against the landlords who had been exploiting them, but the strength was not only of the poor tribes, but also learned people joined the movement.

The state of Jharkhand was carved out from the southern part of Bihar on 15th November 2000, as the 28th state of the Indian Union. It inherited the menace of Maoism, which till date has noticed numerous naxal insurgencies. In the year 2008, the Prime Minister termed Left Wing extremism as a big security threat to the nation. In response, counter naxal trends have also been experienced and are still among the solutions. But much of these activities have led to even greater violations of human rights. Poor people of the villages are often forced to support the squads. The naxals carry on their activities in the name of the poor, downtrodden, and, tribal people. But the groups have now been known for their greed of levy extraction from various sources, from development programs, Corporate. Much of the squads now behave as other criminal groups.

The state of Jharkhand has for most of its period, had unstable government. The development works only have mentions on paper and rarely are accomplished honestly. Corruption remains at heights and most of the ministers have criminal background. In such situations, naxalism adds up to the worse conditions and the problem now seeks a sustainable solution.

The three pronged solution of: Social and economic development, multi-lateral dialogue and military force- need to be focused. In coming up with strategies for national economic growth, the government must always bear in mind the possible effects of fast growth for all socio-economic groups in a country as large and diverse as India.

Former President APJ Abdul Kalam on views on Naxalism, highlighted on the fact that Maoism is prevalent in the areas where land reforms had not been successful. He stressed on to bring inclusive land reforms in these areas. Another thing that he emphasized is lending of earning capacity to every person. People also become part of naxal cadres, after being frustrated from unemployment and inaccessibleness to profitable income. PURA (Providing Urban Amenities in Rural Areas) according to him can be of great help. Employment programs ought to be made free from their unwanted drawbacks.

Non-egalitarian conditions have been the causes for evolution of Maoism. The Gandhian approach can be solution to the vulnerable situations. The participation of people in governance and development according to their own immediate demands can lead to peaceful conditions. The state machineries and its efficiency need to be improved. Rights of each should be made available. Also among the solutions, monopoly of the corporate houses should be put to limits. Washing out of the menace of Naxalism is impossible even for military efforts or for any government without it. "Violence cannot be ended through violence/'

Chapter – II

Maoism: Ideological and International Outlook

In the earlier phases of tribal and regional movements, the revolutionary communist groups had gained success. However, the movement when reached a certain phase in its development, a mid group was noted to part away from the main. Similar consequences had been observed in Nepal after the elections, the parted groups being exposed of their intensions. These splits have been consequences of difference between the principles of each splinter groups that evolved through time. The democratic environment does not lend space for ideologies like Maoism to spread its wings in a nation like India. Every ideology itself fades away through whirls of era. Despite of the various criticisms, the state provides much independence through its political system, that of multiple party existence. In such situations, groups like the Left Wing Extremists cannot have legitimate existence. The Communists themselves have experienced most successes through ways of open elections.

The bloody violence in the states has resulted in anger against the extremists. In midst of all these, the government in India sponsored ways to counter Naxalism, through armed forces too. But the most important point that needs consideration is that, areas under menace are under developed, economically, socially and politically. The people of these areas in some or the other way find themselves in different developmental positions than in other states. The governments cannot justify its effective working in such conditions. Prime Minister and the Home Minister have already declared counter naxalism among the main aims of the government.

Ideological and Political Perspective

In terms of its ideological and political nature, Mao Zedong's ideology is said to be an interpretation of Marxist and Leninist theory of Communalism. With the evolution of Mao Zedong's idea, it also gained popularity in some other nations. During the 1960s, the" differences between the Communist Party of the then Soviet Union and Communist Party of China resulted in splits among various communist parties of nations throughout the world. The followers of Mao's Communist Party of China, declared Mao's principles as the main theme for their movements in their own countries. These groups came to be known as the Marxist-Leninist (ML) groups. Around 36 such groups were then found in all over the world. Other than some exceptions, leaders and workers who formed the splinted Marxist-Leninist groups were in limited numbers, and so were the groups- small. The splits also influenced many independence movements of nations. Groups emerged with motives of mobilizing the peasants and labor classes on the basis of Mao's ideologies in semi feudal and semi capitalist societies of Asia, Africa and Latin America, through guerilla warfare with aims of bringing revolutions. Such were the uprisings of Naxalbari of May 1967 and the armed struggles sponsored by the CPI(ML) of 22nd April 1969. In 1966, Mao Zedong organised the Cultural Revolution by the Proletariats. The main thought behind, was that even in Socialist societies, inequality persisted between classes. Still a conflict existed between the Socialist and Capitalist societies. Mao gave the slogan, "Bombard the Bourgeois Headquarters." Many leaders of the Communist Party of China, even the then Head of the State of China, Liu Shaoqi, and Deng Xiaoping, chairman of CCP were sent to prison. Several leaders and party workers were sent for re education. Many people were put to hostile situations and many were detained and killed. This revolution went on in China for about ten years. Many Marxist- Leninist, Mao's theory based Communist parties were keen supporters of the Proletariat Cultural Revolution. Countries began to have their Red Guard troops on the lines of China's Red Guards. With passage of time however, in some countries the revolts led by the Marxist-Leninist groups began to weaken. Till the decade of 70s, the movements in Vietnam and China which had been an encouraging revolt for Communist parties of the world also weakened. Mao Zedong died on 9th September 1976. The ten years old Cultural Revolution of China was also declared to have come to a halt. With the resettlement of Deng Xiaoping, a new phase of economic improvement started. In reality the Cultural Revolution of Mao had been a failure in destroying the Bourgeois Headquarters, which had again regained its power from 1978. Liu Shaoqi also gained the prestige again. The Cultural Revolution was declared disastrous for development of the nation. Mao though officially is regarded as the great revolutionary in the CPC for creating the People's Republic of China, but Maoism as implemented between 1959 and 1976 is regarded by today's CPC as an economic and political disaster. Till the end of 1980s, the Cultural Revolution and the arguments of 1960s, was being considered a fraud in China. The importance had only remained in terms of relations between China and Russia. The Communist Party of China had separated itself from the parties with Mao's ideologies. And was busy in liaise with parties having intentions of friendly relations with nations. The Berlin Wall was demolished in 1989. Within two years, Soviet Union's 1917 October revolution's ideologies had faded away and capitalists had got a hold. Much of the

Marxist-Leninist Communist parties (on Mao's ideologies), till the end of the decade of 1980s had either lost its base or had begun to adopt the path of open elections and democratic means to retain its existence. The Marxist-Leninist parties earlier too had existence in only a few countries.

In the earlier phases of tribal and regional movements, the revolutionary communist groups have gained success. However, the movement when reached a certain phase in its development, a mid group was noted to have parted from the main. Similar consequences had been observed in Nepal after the elections, the parted groups being exposed of their intensions. The Nepal Communist Party's differentiated in its thoughts from that of COMPOSA. However, the society in Nepal itself has been in an evolving period, from feudal to capitalist and democratic society. The democratic environment does not lend much space for ideologies like Maoism. But in Nepal, the Communist party with Mao's ideology gained much success. In the earliest phase too, the Nepal Communist Party was the strongest amongst all. Instead of interpreting Mao's ideology in terms of Lenin's theories, the Maoists and their aims have departed from the true Marxist and Leninist ideology. According to them, the semi feudal and semi imperial societies in most of the countries of the Third World leave much space for their ideology. The need according to them is of a political party and armed leadership towards the movement. The Maoists consider the post Mao Zedong's China, a capitalist society. In this sense, the Communist Party in Peru, Latin America, also known as the Shining Path is credited with Maoist following. A communist squad in Nepal, started experimenting the Mao's ideology from 1966. The Maoist Communist Centre(MCC) had been active since 1969, this group since then had been a critic of the formation of the Marxist-Leninist group. The Revolutionary Internationalist Movement was formed on 12th March 1984. In its initial period, it consisted of nineteen Maoist groups. Later it went down to thirteen. In the year 1991, the Nepal Communist Party (Maoist) was reestablished. In the midst of 1990s, the Central Committee of the party decided to launch a long term war, was initiated on 13th February 1996. Till this time, the Communist party of Peru had disintegrated. And Gonzalo had been detained. Till now Nepal had emerged as the main RIMS and communist basis instead of Peru. The South Asian Maoist parties and associations formed The Coordination Committee of Maoist Parties and Organisations of South Asia (CCOMPOSA), on 21st July 2001. Among the constituent parties were the Communist Party of Nepal (Maoist), Communist Party of India (Marxist-Leninist), Maoist Communist Centre of India, Revolutionary Communist Centre of India (Marxist-Leninist-Maoist), Revolutionary Communist Centre of India (Maoist), and Communist Party of India (Marxist-Leninist) People's War. The Ceylon Communist Party (Maoist) of Sri Lanka, Purba Bangala Sarbahara Party (Central Committee), Purba Bangla Sarbahara Party (Maobadi Punargathan Kendra), Bangladesher Samyabadi Dal (Marksbadi-Leninbadi), Purba Banglar Communist Party - Marksbadi-Leninbadi (Lal Patakar), Purba Banglar Sarbahara Party (Maoist Bolshevik Reorganisation Movement), and Bhutan Communist Party (Marxist-Leninist-Maoist) were given the observer status. Under the 1985 Bhutan Citizenship Act, around 150000 Nepali speaking Bhutanese people were declared non citizens and were evicted from Bhutan. These refugees resided in Eastern Nepal, in various camps. With the efforts of Nepali Maoists, The Bhutan Communist Party (Marxist-Leninist-Maoist) was introduced. Other than these, the RIMS consisted of Communist Party of Peru, The Revolutionist Party of America, and parties of Turkey, Iran and among other, Philippines. Belgium's Worker Party is also said to have concerns. Nevertheless, the Maoist Party of Nepal was the biggest and other parties except that of Peru, India and Philippines were quite small groups. The most benefitted from the activities obviously were the Maoists of Nepal.

(*Source:* "Naxalwad, Sawalon Ke Katghare Mein" by-Prasann Kumar Choudhary)

Naxalism: Indian Perspectives

Revolutionaries from before (1925) had repudiated and resisted the so called opportunitism, revisionism, and treachery of the Communist Party of India as well of the CPI (M). But the struggle between the correct and the erroneous lines intensified in the 1960s, when Mao Zedong and the Communist Party of China launched the debate against the modern revisionism, and the eruption of the Great Prolitariat Cultural Revolution (GPCR from 1966-1976.

Influenced and guided by the principles propagated by the GPCR, these revolutionaries in India started following the Marxist-Leninist-Mao Zedong's path for development in the country too. This resulted in break from the old party, of a large number of cadres and declaration of 7th congress, and the entire leadership of the Communist Party of India (Marxist) revisionist. Cheru Mazumdar was one of the active cadres, became the founder of the Communist Party of India (Marxist-Leninist). He declared the peoples war as the right path towards revolution, against that of the parliamentary system, followed by the CPI (Marxist).

In India, a sort of communist movement was initiated earlier in July 1948 by the Telangana struggle, in which 2500 villages of south were organised as peasant movement. The Andhra Thesis for the first time had made a demand to follow the path of protracted peoples war of China,for the Indian revolution too. In the same year, the leftist ideological document, Andhra Letter laid a strategy for the Indian revolution based on Mao Zedong's ideology. It was first in 1964 that the CPM split from the United CPI and decided to participate in the elections. Thus postponing arm struggle over revolutionary policies. Cheru Majumdar's writings on Marx-Lenin-Mao thoughts, of 1965-66 became popular as the Historic Eight Documents and became influensive for the Naxal movement. In 1967, the United Front Government, a collision government by CPM and Bangla Congress was formed in West Bengal. This led to withdrawal on basis of doctrinal grounds, in the party by younger cadres including Cheru Majumdar, accusing CPM of betraying the revolution.

The rebel cadres led by Cheru Majumdar in Naxalbari of the Darjeeling district on 25th May 1967, a peasants' uprising grew as a revolt against the attack by the local Goons of the landlords on 2nd March on a tribal youth who had the judicial order to plough his land. Tribals retaliated by forcefully capturing back their land. This incidence known as the "Clarion Call of Spring Thunder", signaled a new revolutionary path in the Indian context. This also gave the name "Naxalide" or "Maoist" to the cadres who bolted the CPI, towards the new path of revolution.

The CPI (M) led United Front government cracked down on the uprising, within 72 days of the uprising, a sub inspector and 9 tribals were killed. The central government of Congress supported the crackdown. The whole incidence echoed throughout the country and Naxalism was born.

The ideology of Naxalism started gaining larger dimensions and the state units of the CPI(M) in Uttar Pradesh, Jammu Kashmir and some parts of Bihar and Andhra Pradesh joined the struggle. After the Naxalbari uprising, some revolutionaries began to have different views on how to advance people's war in India and whether it was timely to establish a new party. These conflicts were not immediately resolved. Also because of this, the CPI (ML) led by Comrade Cheru Mazumdar was established on April 22,1969, separately from the Maoist Communist Center of India (MCCI) led by Comrade Kanai Chatterjee which was founded on October 20,1969. The two organisations' development was interrupted several times due to various factors, such as the martyrdom of Cheru Mazumdar and the capture and detention of Kanai Chatterjee, among other problems.

Earlier to this, on November 12th to 13th of 1967, comrades from Tamil Nadu, Kerala, Uttar Pradesh, Bihar, Karnataka, and West Bengal had met to form the All India Coordination Committee of Revolutionaries (AICCR). in the CPI(M). According to the decision of the AICCCR, a new party, the CPI(ML) was formed on the birth anniversary of Lenin on 22nd April1969. Cheru Majumndar was elected the secretary of the Central Organizing Committee and AICCR dissolved itself. Armed clash for the first time occurred between the cadres of CPI (M) and CPI(ML) initiated by the disruption of the meeting at which Kanu Sanyal made a declaration on party formation in the Shahid Minar ground in Calcutta. By this time primary guerrilla zone appeared at Debra-gopiballavpur (WB), Musal in Bihar, Lakhimpur Kheri in UP and most importantly Srikakulam in Andhra Pradesh.

Central Bihar and Telangana saw fresh Guerrilla struggles in 1973. The ultra leftist movement suffered suppressions resulting from the declaration of emergency of 25th June 1975, and the Central Organizing Committee in its September meeting decided to withdraw the "common self critical review" and instead produce a tactical line, road to revolution. But it did not bring unity among the cadres. Armed struggles were reported from Bhojpur and Naxalbari. 1976-CPI (ML) held its second Congress on February 26-27 in the countryside of Gaya, in Bihar. It resolved to continue with armed guerilla struggles and work for an anti-Congress United Front. In 1978 rectification movements (CPI ML and fragments) limited pure military viewpoint and stressed mass peasant struggles to Indianise the Marxism-Leninism and Mao thought. CPI (ML) (Unity Organisation) was formed in Bihar under N. Prasad's leadership focusing on Jehanabad-Palamu. A peasant organisation - the Mazdoor

Kisan Sangram Samiti (MKSS) was also formed. Between 1979 to 1988, MCC focused on Bihar. A Bihar-Bengal Special Area Committee was established. The Preparatory Committee for Revolutionary Peasant Struggles was formed and soon Revolutionary Peasant Councils emerged. There was a will to form a unified core central organisation representing the central core democratic front, resulted in the organisation of unity meet of 13 factions of the Marxist-Leninist in 1981. But this effort did not go successful. The M-L movement began to polarize between the Marxist-Leninist line of CPI (ML) (Liberation) and the line of CPI (ML) (People's War). The PWG and the MCC were banned by the Bihar government in 1986.

In 1980, the CPI (ML) had split into two camps—the CPI (ML)-People's War that based itself in Andhra Pradesh and Tamil Nadu; and the CPI (ML) People's Unity that operated in Bengal. Despite the split, cadres continued their efforts to unite the similar but splintered groups. In 1998, the CPI (ML) [PW] and the CPI (ML) [PU] formally merged under the name CPI-(ML) [PW].

The efforts for unification continued between CPI (ML) (PW) and MCCI that mainly was based in Bengal, on firm political and theoretical aspects, and in accordance with correct military line. But the attempts to unite from 1985 to 1995 failed and the complicated bitter relations between the two also grew bloody.

However in the meeting of 2003, the two groups opened themselves to criticisms and let their weaknesses lessen through discussions on issues, political and revolutionary. This then resulted in drafting of the foundation documents for the formation of the merged group- CPI(Maoist) which was formed on 1st September 2004. According to the merged party, "the establishment of the merger party was in accordance with the desires and demands of the toiling masses for a genuine party of the proletariat that would lead revolutionary change for the establishment of a new democratic society towards socialism and communism." The emergence of the guerilla armies of the two parties were also done to form the united People's Liberation Guerilla Army (PLGA).

(*Source:* "Naxalism in Jharkhand" by EPS (Retd.) Bimal Kishore Sinha; and PRWC: Introduction to Indian society and revolution, Ang Bayan, 19 July 2013 - philippinerevolution.net)

THE RED CORRIDOR

LEFT-WING EXTREMIST AFFECTED AREAS IN INDIA

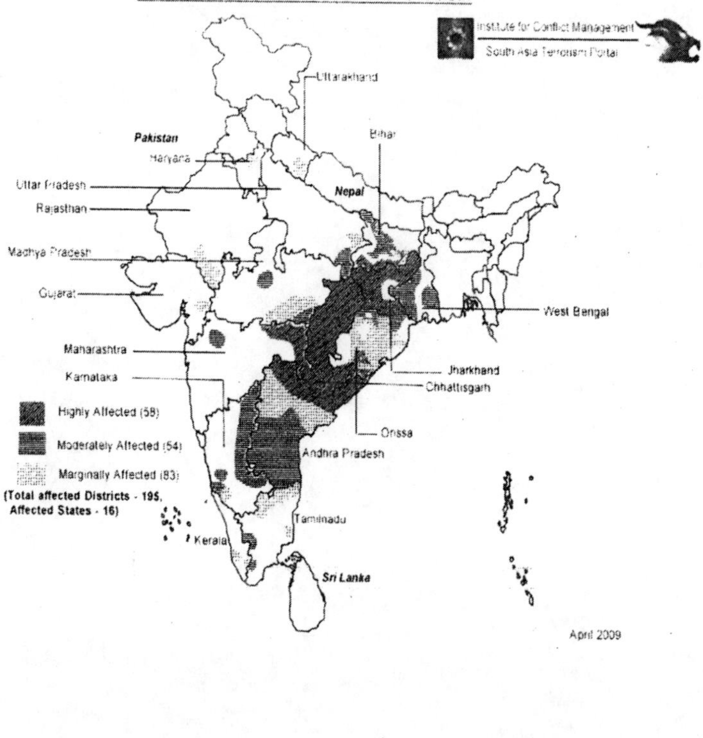

Chapter – III

Naxal Incidences in Jharkhand

Jharkhand together with Chhattisgarh and Bihar accounts for around 80 per cent (highest) of the left wing extremists' violence throughout the country. Jharkhand fared with highest number of incidences of naxal violence in the first quarter of this year. It has also consolidated its lead over Chhattisgarh in this regard, when its incidences grew to twice and deaths to thrice of that of Chhattisgarh. Though this period of first quarter of the year records a fall down in the number of incidences and deaths, if compared with that of the previous year (from 417 in March 2012 to 272 incidences in March 2013 and from 120 in March 2012 to 89 deaths till the same period of 2013); Jharkhand with highest Naxal attacks is a matter to worry for. With these numbers, the state accounted to 40 per cent of the Naxal incidences all over India and to 58 per cent of deaths till March of this year. It is since 2011, that Jharkhand has left all the other states behind in this concern. Of the 52 deaths in Jharkhand, 37 civilians were killed and 14of them were killed after being branded informers of police; and 25 from the security forces.

In matters of counter Naxal activities, killings by security forces also up to some extend show increase in this period of first three months of 2013, which increased to 18 in comparison to 14 in the first three months of the last year. Jharkhand ranked third in this regard, after Chhattisgarh and Maharashtra. Out of 167 of the total arms recovery, 60 had been done in Jharkhand.

(Source: "Jharkhand records highest Naxal violence this year"- Times Of India articles.timesofindia.indiatimes.com >)

The number of incidences of naxal violence in the country has reduced, but in case of state of Jharkhand, a modest reduction in such incidences has been recorded. The data from Union Ministry of Home Affairs confirm this. According to MHA total fatalities in Jharkhand declined by under 14 per cent, from 198 in 2011, to 169 in 2012, while all-India fatalities declined from 710 to 488, a drop of over 31 per cent. 133 civilians were killed in 2012, though the number was down from 149 in 2011. Chhattisgarh, the State recording the second highest civilian fatalities, registered 63 killed, less than half the number for Jharkhand. SF and Maoist fatalities also declined marginally, from 33 and 16, respectively, in 2011, to 29 and seven in 2012. Partial data compiled by the South Asia Terrorism Portal (SATP) records a total of 20 Maoist related fatalities in Jharkhand in 2013 (till January 27), including six civilians, 10 SF personnel and 4 Maoists.

Fatalities in LWE/CPI-Maoist Violence in Jharkhand and All India; 2011-2012

Years	*2011*				*2012*			
Category	**Civilian**	**SFs**	**LWEs**	**Total**	**Civilian**	**SFs**	**LWEs**	**Total**
Jharkhand	149	33	16	198	133	29	7	169
All India	469	142	99	710	300	114	74	488

Source: MHA.

The following table highlights some other parameters of Left Wing Extremist/CPI-Maoist violence in 2011 and 2012.

Other Parameters of LWE/CPI-Maoist Violence in Jharkhand: 2011-2012

Parameters	***2011***	***2012***
No. of incidents	517	479
Police Informers' Killed (Out of total civilians killed)	35	32
No. of encounters with police	42	43
No. of attacks on police (including landmines)	23	21
No. of Naxalites arrested	380	377
No. of Naxalites surrendered	17	6
Total no. of arms snatched	17	30
Total no. of arms recovered	185	162
Arms training camps held .	24	12
No of Jan Adalats held	54	23

Source: MHA.

The table below presents quantitative data and nature of incidents of Attacks on Economic Targets by LWE-Extremists in Jharkhand: 2008-2012.

Incidents of Attacks on Economic Targets by LWE Extremists in Jharkhand: 2008-2012

	2008	***2009***	***2010***	***2011***	***2012***
Railways	7	17	13	10	2
Telephone Exchange	10	14	6	8	3
Mining	4	2	6	2	0
Pole transmission	0	0	1	0	0
Panchayat Bhawan	0	7	4	0	1
School Building	4	37	7	6	0

Source: Source: MHA.

According to partial data compiled by SATP, incidents of killing (civilian, SF and Naxal) were reported from 14 Districts in 2012 - Bokaro (1), Chatra (5), Dhanbad (1) Garhwa (13) Giridih (8) Gumla (18) Hazaribagh (3) Khunti (13) Latehar (12) Pakur (1) Palamu (7) Ranchi (6) Simdega (5) and West Singhbhum (5).

In 2011 incidents of killing were recorded in 16 Districts.

Among the other patterns of violence recorded by SATP, the Maoists engaged in 18 incidents of arson in 11 Districts - Khunti (3), Giridih (2), Lohardaga (2), Ranchi (2), Latehar (2), West Singhbhum (2), Chatra (1), Gumla (1), Dumka (1), Bokaro (1) and Garwah (1).

Emphasizing these incidents, Director General of Police (DGP) G.S. Rath, on December 20, 2012, stated that, barring incidents of setting ablaze of vehicles, Maoist activities have been 'contained to a large extent' in Jharkhand. LWE groups also abducted at least 26 Persons through 2012, and triggered at least 9 landmine blasts in the State. Jharkhand recorded at least six major incidents (involving three or more fatalities) against 14 such incidents in 2011.

An analysis of Maoist violence, as well as of overground and underground activities, through 2012, indicates that Bokaro, Chatra, Dhanbad, Garhwa, Giridih, Gumla, Hazaribagh, Khunti, Latehar, Pakur, Palamu, Ranchi, Simdega and West Singhbhum Districts remain highly affected; while Dhanbad, Lohardaga and Ramgarh are moderately affected.

Along with the CPI-Maoist, other splinter groups (which have broken away from the CPI-Maoist) continue to operate. These groups include the People's Liberation Front of India (PLFI), Tritiya Prastuti Committee (TPC), Jharkhand Prastuti Committee (JPC), Jharkhand Janmukti Parishad (JJP), Swatantra Jan Sangharsh India Morcha (SJSIM), Sangharsh Janmukti Morcha (SJMM), and Jharkhand Sangharsh Janmukti Morcha (JSJM). These splinter groups are strongly antagonist to CPI-Maoist though they also fight among themselves. On June 24, 2012, in a change of strategy, the CPI-Maoist decided to call off violence against other armed outfits, including their splinter groups, for three months, to facilitate unity of action against the unified command of the Centre and the State Governments. The attempt, however, appears to have failed.

Significantly, S.N. Pradhan, the Jharkhand Police spokesperson, disclosed to the media that none of the 23 troopers who died in encounters in 2012 (till October), had been killed by non-Maoist groups. On the other hand, of the 33 extremists killed during this period in Jharkhand, 22 were reportedly eliminated in fratricidal operations by rival groups. Six died in encounters with Government Forces, while five were lynched by the "public". In 2011, fratricidal violence reportedly killed 40 Maoists. CPI-Maoist involvement in violent incidents came down from 65-70 per cent in 2008-09 to 44 per cent in 2012, S. N. Pradhan added. In contrast, the PLFI's 'share' rose to 30 per cent, from 14 per cent. He observed, further, "Where the (CPI) Maoists are retreating, their rival groups are moving in to occupy the space. All of them are purely criminal groups fighting over extortion and killing people if their demands are not met."

(*Source:* "Maoist: Jharkhand Assessment 2013 - South Asia Terrorism Portal" www.satp.org/satporgtp/countries/india/.../Assessment/.../Jharkhand.htm)

Jharkhand Map

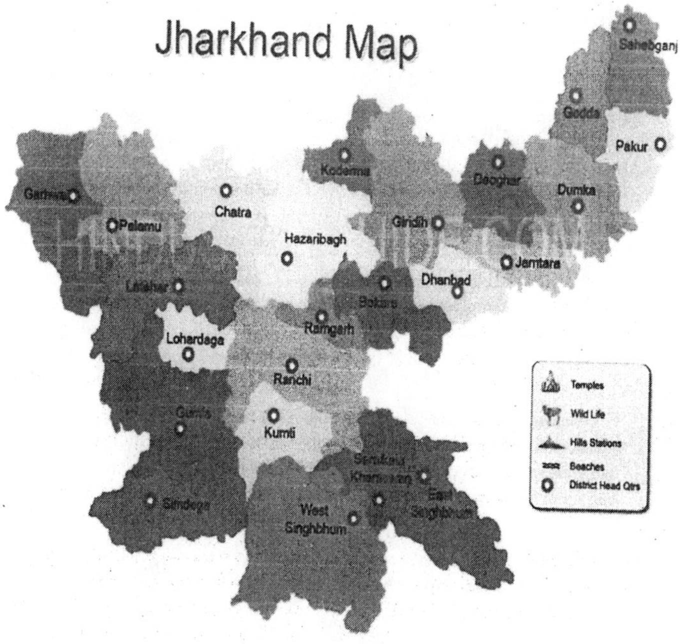

Chapter – IV

Jharkhand

The state of Jharkhand, popularly known as Vananchal (land of woods), is located in the eastern part of India. With an area of 79,714 sq km, the state shares its border with Bihar in the north, Uttar Pradesh and Chhattisgarh in the west, Orissa in the south, and West Bengal in the east. The state has been gifted with its rich mineral reserves and hosts much of the country's largest industrial units such as the Bokaro Steel plant, which is the largest steel plant in Asia; India's first iron and steel factory in Jamshedpur and many others. The rivers flowing through the state, play an important role in the socio-economic aspects of the society.

Jharkhand, being a mineral rich state, is among the most industrialised regions in the country, it accounts for 35.5 per cent of the country's known coal reserves, 90 per cent of its cooking coal deposits, 40 per cent of its copper, 22 per cent of its iron ore, 90 per cent of its mica and huge deposits of bauxite, quartz and ceramics.

"According to the India State of Forest Report 2011, the forest cover in the state, based on interpretation of satellite data of November 2008-January 2009 is 22,977 sq km, which is 28.82 per cent of the state's geographical area. In terms of forest canopy density classes, the state has 2,590 sq km area under very dense forest, 9,917 sq km area under moderately dense forest and 10,470 sq km area under open forest."

The rich forests and natural resources contributed to 70% of the undivided Bihar's domestic product. Despite this, it is still one of the most backward states in India with its per capita Net State Domestic Product (INR 22,780) well below the national average (INR 33,731) and Net Domestic Product growth rate of 6.35 per cent which is below the national average.

(*Source:* About Jharkhand I UNDP
www.undp.org/content/india/en/home/..Jharkhand/about-Jharkhand)

The state of Jharkhand was carved out of the southern part of Bihar on 15th of November 2000.

The name: Jharkhand" means "the land of forests". The state accounts for 40 per cent of the total mineral resources of India. Ranchi accounts for 50 per cent of the mineral production of the state and around 18 per cent of the mineral production of the country.

According to some writers, Jharkhand as a geo political, cultural identity existed since after the period of Magadha empire. According to a Hindu mythological book, the tribal rulers were known as the Munda Rajas, some of whom continue to thrive till today. These people basically had ownership rights to large farm lands. The region came to be known as Kukara during the Mughal period.

After 1765, it came under British rule and came to be known as Jharkhand- the worship place of Kherwar(Munda, Santhal, Ho), and Khonds. Jharkhand is located on Chota Nagpur Plateau and Santhal Parganas. It has evergreen forests, rolling hills, and rocky plateaus.

The Adivasis of Jharkhand had actively participated in series of revolts against British rule, from much before the revolt of 1857. The period from 1771 to 1900, was marked by revolts by tribals to protect Jharkhand land. The first such revolt was lead by Tilka Manjhi, Santhal leader of Santhal belt in 1971. This revolt against the landlords was crushed by the British troops. Followed after this however were struggles such as that of 1779, by the Bhumij tribe against British rule in Manbhum, now in West Bengal; that of 1800, by the Chero tribes in Palamu. The murder of landlord in Srinagar, west of Gumla in 1807, spread the struggle to around Gumla and eastward to the neighbouring Temar areas of Munda tribes, and then were seen the struggles of 1811 and 1813. The Lakra Coal risings were led by Hos of Singhbhum in 1820-1821 against the landlords and British troops. The big revolt, the 1932 Coal Risings was excited by the zamindars when they tried to oust the tribal peasants from their hereditary possessions. The Santhal Rebellion of 1855 led by Siddho and Kanu is well known, but was crushed by the British troops. The Birsa Munda revolt broke out in 1895 and lasted till 1900. The revolt though mainly concentrated in the Munda belt of Khunti, Tamar, Sarwada and Bandgaon, pulled its supporters from Oraon belt of Lohardaga, Sisai and even Barway. It was the longest and the greatest tribal revolt.

The division of Chota Nagpur had experienced many of the revolts, but they were suppressed and the area became the victim of British policy of "divide and rule". Some princely states were transferred to Orissa division by Lord Curzon in 1905 together with the partition of Bengal and some other princely states to Chhattisgarh division of Central Provinces. At the time of unification of Bengal in 1912, the Bihar division, Chota Nagpur division, and the Orissa division were taken out and Orissa was formed at the time of Governor General Lord Harding. Midnapur, Purulia and Bankura remained with Bengal. At each time of reorganisation, Chota Nagpur lost some region. Tribal areas though geographically continuous, were put under different administrative areas. After independence, by the act of accession of princely states to the government of India, princely states of Magadha was added to Orissa province; that of Jashpur, Surguja, Udaipur, Chang Bhakar and Koriya were put under. Madhya Pradesh and Midnapur; Purulia and Bankura were put under West Bengal. Princely states of Gangpur and Bonai were combined together to form Sundergarh District. Princely states of Koriya and Chang bhakar were combined together to form Koriya district and Udaipur were included in Raigarh District.

In comparison to the revolts of the 19th century, the revolts of 20th century were moderate. With the upcoming of the Chotanagpur Tenancy Act of 1908 for the protection of lands, the tribals now moved towards the socio-economic demands. The Tana movement of 1914 led by the Chatra Oraons later in 1920 joined the Gandhian Satyagraha, resisted by not giving taxes to the government. The Chotanagpur Unnati Samaj was set up in 1915 for social and economic development of the tribal people, the group also had political objectives. In the year 1928, it placed demand for a separate state of Jharkhand with self rule by the tribals before the Simon Commission in Patna, which however was not accepted. In the year 1935, the Chotanagpur Unnati Samaj and the Kishan Sabha(of 1931) merged together to form to gain political power.

After Independence, the Jharkhand Party made continuous efforts for the formation of a separate state of Jharkhand. In spite of its political strength, the demands for the state were rejected one after one by the commissions established to examine the demands, sometime after not accepting such a demand for benefit of tribals and sometimes rejecting on linguistic grounds. Though the Jharkhand Party didn't give up with the demand, after 1962 when the party allied with Congress and the political interests of leaders grew during the elections the demand came to a freeze for almost a decade.

In the 4th General Election held in 1967 the party couldn't perform well. It could win only eight Assembly seats.

The party was soon split into several splinter groups each claiming to be the genuine Jharkhand party. These were the All India Jharkhand Party led by Bagun Sumroi, the Jharkhand Party led by N.E. Horo, the Hul Jharkhand Party led by Justin Richard which got further fragmented and came to be called the Bihar Progressive Hul Jharkhand Party and it was led by Shibu Soren. The movement was infused with a new radicalism when Santhal leader Shibu Soren formed the Jharkhand Mukti Morcha (JMM) in league with the Marxist co-ordination Committee in 1972. In its early years, the JMM under Soren's leadership, brought industrial and mining workers mainly non-tribals belonging to Dalit and Backward communities such as Surdis, Doms, Dusadh and Kurmi-Mahtos, into its fold. However Soren's association with the late congress M.P. Gyanranjan brought him close to then prime minister of India, Indira Gandhi, in New Delhi. He won the Dumka Lok Sabha seat in 1972. Irked by Soren's association with the Congress, a few of the younger members of the JMM banded together in Jamshedpur and set up the All Jharkhand Students' Union (AJSU). This did nothing to stunt the growth of the JMM in the 1991 Lok Sabha election where the JMM won six seats.

Another foreign educated scholar, Ram Dayal Munda, reignited the movement by unifying splinter groups among the tribals. Under his guidance the Jharkahnd Coordination Committee was constituted in June 1987, comprising 48 organisations and group including the JMM factions. Due to Munda, Soren, Mandal and AJSU leaders like Surya Singh Besra and Prabhakar Tirkey briefly shared a political platform. But the JMM withdrew from JCC. The JMM/AJSU and JPP successfully orchestrated bandhs, economic blockades in 1988-89. In the interim, BJP came out with its demand for a separate "Vananchal" state comprising 18 districts of Bihar, arguing that demand for a greater Jharkhand is "not practical". In response, Buta Singh, the then home minister, asked Ram Dayal Munda, the then Ranchi University vice chancellor, to prepare a report on

Jharkhand. Munda handed his report in September 1988, advising the Home Ministry to grant 'autonomy' to 'Greater Jharkhand'. In August 1989, the Union Home Ministry formed a committee on Jharkhand Matters (CoJM) to look into the issue. These were followed by further talks between the then Bihar Chief Minister, Satyendra Narayan Sinha, the central government and Jharkhand groups. In September 1989 the COJM submitted its report proposing the alternatives to the formation of a greater Jharkhand, a Union Territory or a Jharkhand general council. In 1995 the Jharkhand Area Autonomous Council (JAAC) was set up after a tripartite agreement was signed by the Union government represented by the then minister of state for home, Rajesh Pilot, the Bihar government represented by the chief minister Lalu Prasad Yadav and Jharkhand leaders like Soren, Munda, Mandal, Besra and Tirkey. Horo did not sign this agreement. He dubbed the JAAC as the 'fraud' and stuck to his demand for Tribal Homeland. So did the AJSU and JPP.

Finally, it was on 15th November 2000 that the Jharkhand state was formed as the 28th state of the Indian union, and to protect a Jharkhandi identity for the tribal people. The correct interpretation would however be that the new state with and aim to provide autonomous power and identity to the tribes, was the result of the failure to intervene in the social and economic development of the Advisees and non Adivasis, and not specifically for premising the unique tribal heritage and culture. The state was carved out of the underdeveloped part of the south Bihar. Socio economic structures still depend on the dynamics of resource and political development.

(*Source:* en.wikipedia.org/wiki/Jharkhand)

Districts in Jharkhand

Jharkhand has 24 administrative districts. Originally, it had 18 districts at the time of its formation. 6 more districts were added to the list by carving out more from these by reorganisation. The 23rd and 24th districts of Ramgarh and Khunti came into existence on 7th September 2007.

Presently the 24 districts are divided into 5 divisions namely, Palamu division(headquarters-Medininagar), North Chotanagpur division(headquarters-Hazaribagh), South Chotanagpur division(headquarters-Ranchi), Kolhan division(headquarters-Chaibasa),and Santhal Pargana division(headquarters-Dumka.

The districts presently in existence are: Garhwa, Palamu, Latehar, Chatra, Hazaribagh, Koderma, Giridih, Ramgarh, Bokaro, Dhanbad, Lohardaga, Gumla, Simdega, Ranchi, Khunti, West Singhbhum, Saraikela Kharsawan, East Singhbhum, Jamtara, Deoghar, Dumka, Pakur, Godda, and Sahebganj.

(*Source:* en.wikipedia.org/wiki/List and www.traveliharkhand.com/iharkhand-tourism/districts-in-iharkhand.html)

Jharkhand has met a population growth of 22.4 per cent. But the tribal population itself has lessen down by 0.1 per cent. According to the Primary Census Abstract 2011, the total population in the state as on March 1, 2011, was 3,29,88,134. In absolute number, total population surge in 2011, as compared to 2001, was 60,42,305. Of this, 76 per cent reside in rural areas and 24 per cent in the urban regions. "The population of scheduled tribe was 86,45,042. Of them, 78,68,150 live in rural and 7,76,892 in urban areas. In terms of proportion, scheduled tribe population constitutes 26.2 per cent (rural 31.4 per cent and urban 9.8 per cent). The proportion during Census 2001 was 26.3 per cent. There has been a decrease of 0.1 per cent during the last decade." The 73.3 per cent of the tribals in Khunti accounts for the highest schedule tribal population in the state; whereas Kodarma has only 1 per cent of schedule tribe population that is the lowest percentage in Jharkhand. The scheduled caste population showed marginal increase of 0.3 per cent in the last one decade. The total scheduled caste population in the state was 39,85,644. Of them, 31,52,863 is in rural area and 8,32,781 in urban centres. The proportion of scheduled caste population in the state is 12.1 per cent as against 11,8 per cent in 2011. Jharkhand has a population density of 414. Dhanbad has the highest population density at 1,316 people per sqkm and Simdega the lowest with just 159.

The reduction in the tribal population can be attributed to a number of factors such as rising industrialisation, urbanisation, low birth rate and high death rate among tribals, immigration of non-tribal communities in the region and emigration of tribal people to other places.

(*Source:* Marginal fall in tribal population in Jharkhand - Times Of India articles.timesofindia.indiatimes.com) >

Chapter – V

Naxalism in Jharkhand: Historical-overview

In The areas of Bihar and Jharkhand, the Maoist Communist Centre of lndia)MCCI) and the Communist Party of India, Marxist- Leninist(People's War) had been putting great influence as the communist terrorist groups, and the violence gained new peaks since its merge in September 2004. The parties before this period too were influential enough, so much so that 88 per cent of the total violence in the country and 90 per cent of total deaths had been the consequences. The merged party, CPI (Maoist), has led to new records of incidences, more violent, more injurious, and more harmful to the states. The document named "Naxalite Movement in Bihar and Jharkhand" of April 2005 specified 150 deaths against 117 in 18 districts out of the then 22 districts of Jharkhand bringing the state to second in its rank in terms of Naxal killings. The success of Maoism in Nepal and activities of the various front organisations has been influencing.

Before the division of Jharkhand from Bihar in November 2000, it was assumed that the non tribal political leaders and bureaucratic officials were least concerned for the tribal development. A new government with tribal representatives will work in a better manner for lessening tribal grievances. But this didn't happened, instead the menace of Naxalism penetrated through the district areas of the new created state of Jharkhand and the successive government after the partition seems to have failed in restraining the expansion of the violent extremism. The dense forest cover over large areas of the state provides favorable terrain for their strong bases and naxal operations. The Naxalites have also consolidated their presence in areas bordering Orissa and West Bengal and have been responsible, to a substantial measure, for escalation of Naxalite violence in the neighboring States. Taking advantage of poor coordination among law enforcement agencies between two States, the Naxalites commit crime in one State and slip into the borders of neighboring States. From the year 2001 to 2004 Jharkhand experienced 200, 157, 117, and 150 faculties in the respective successive years. The increase in terror activities has been results of failure of the State governments to address issues contributing to the growth of Naxalism, poor performance of civil administration in rural and tribal areas, ill-equipped police force, and the existence of a collusive arrangement between a section of politicians, bureaucrats/contractors and extremist elements, apart from the strong reason of merge of the two parties and formation of CPI(Maoist) and their increased coordination. Earlier to the unification, the groups often were indulged in bloody wars in parts of Bihar and Jharkhand, due to personal and ideological differences. The intense police operations and large scale use of Prevention of Terrorism Act (POTA) made these group allies.

There also had been instances of linkage of the Naxal groups in the states of Bihar and Jharkhand with Maoists in Nepal. The MCCI and CPI(Maoist)(PW) had such links around 1996 (according to the document "Naxalite Movement in Bihar and Jharkhand"). "Reports in April 2000 informed that the MCC and Maoists were holding joint training camps in Hazaribagh and Aurangabad. In July 2001, the MCC along with the PWG and the Maoists in Nepal, formed an umbrella organisation, the Coordination Committee of Maoist Parties and Organisations of South Asia (CCOMPOSA) to unify and coordinate the activities of the Maoist Parties and organisations in South Asia. All three groups are part of the joint 'Indo-Nepal Border Regional Committee,' and unconfirmed reports indicate that the Indian Naxalite groups have been training Nepali Maoist cadres in various training camps in Bihar and Jharkhand. Apart from the CCOMPOSA, the Revolutionary Internationalist Movement (RIM), which came into existence in 1984, has also been trying to coordinate the activities of Maoist parties in South Asia. Leaders of the RIM are believed to have acted as mediators to strengthen the extreme left in the region."

Among other reasons, the movement has also been conditioned by cast dynamics, political linkage, growing criminalisation, lack of ideological commitment, and turf war over financial resources.

In the initial periods, at British era and also after independence, the insurgencies mainly were promoted at the backdrop of peasant and tribal movements. But with passage of time, it also grew through other local problems which have defined the course of the movement. Issue of land reform, self respect, respect for their women, and payment of minimum wages have been the concerns of these movements in its early phase. The differences between the espousing organisations over strategic, tactical, and organisational aspects resulted in evolution of various naxalite groups in the undivided Bihar.

The movement at Naxalbari of West Bengal had direct impact on top of the then undivided Bihar. The nine member State Committee of Communist Revolutionaries led the activities and spread them to various parts of Bihar. In 1969, the CPI (ML) came into existence. In early 1970s some of its leaders began to establish contacts in Jehanabad and Palamu, but many of them were arrested during emergencies in 1975. Some of them organised the CPI-ML (Unity

Organisation) in 1978, after being released in 1977 during the Janata government's rule. The Mazdur Kisan Sangram Samity (MKSS) was also formed in the same year.

In 1980s, three main groups had influence in Bihar, the CPI-ML (liberation), the CPI-ML(Party Unity), and the MCCI. According to the Bihar government's notes on extremist activities in 1982, out of the 857,47 blocks spread over 14 districts were affected by the left wing extremists' movements. In 1992, the CPI-ML (Liberation) decided to function as an over ground political party. This party had a formidable ground in the central parts of Bihar. It was stated that "the party does not rule out the possibility under a set of exceptional national and international circumstances, the balance of social and economic forces may even permit peaceful transfer of central power to revolutionary forces". It was, however, added that the party must prepare itself for winning the ultimate decisive victory through an armed strugg!e,though it admitted that the situation was not ripe for such a movement. Reports suggest that it still maintains underground squad in some regions. The party also has a string of organisations to mobilize students, women and workers. They are: All India Students Association, Bihar Pradesh Kisan Sabha, All India Coordination Committee of Trade Unions, All India Progressive Women's Association and Jan Sanskritik Manch.

CPI M-L (Party Unity was another group that emerged during 1980s, with peasant mobilizing among its main ways for democratic revolution. It adopted selective annihilation and economic blockade of the land owners amongst its strategies. Towards consolidation, this group merged with the People's War Group (PWG) to form the People's War (PW) in 1998.

The most influential of all has been the MCCI which was earlier known as the Dakshin Desh, was active in putting its impact in West Bengal and Gaya and Hazaribagh. Its work had been to make the peasants realize that land owning was the path to gain political power. Its main concentration grew in Bihar in 1970s and 80s and Bihar Bengal Area Committee was set up. Despite of the suppression during emergency period, in 1978 and 1979 they again started mobilizing the peasants. After being underground till 1982, the MCC began its front activities. In Bihar and Jharkhand, it maintained a string of front organisations, including the Naujawan Pratirodh Sangharsh Manch, Krantikari Budhijivi Sangh, Krantikari Sanskritik Sangh, Krantikari Chhatra League, Communist Yuva League, Naari Mukti Sangh and Mazdoor Mukti Sangh.

MCCs approach was different from that of CPI-ML's of secret killing by the squads. Instead it advocated mass action in which conscious people enraged by class hatred would spontaneously participate in the annihilation of class enemies. Followed were the killings of people mostly from upper casts in parts of today's Bihar and also in Palamu and Hazaribagh.

While on one hand the clashes between cadres of MCCI and CPI-ML (PW) were the phenomena, struggles between CPI-ML(PW) and CPI-ML(Liberation) characterised and influenced the activities.

(*Source:* www.asthabharati.orR/Dia AprQ5/Sanj.htm)

Lights on District Based Uprisings .

At the time of creation of the state of Jharkhand, 8 districts- Palamu, Garhwa, Chatra, Hazaribagh,Giridih Koderma,Lohardagga and Dhanbad were affected with violent naxal activities. The remote areas of Ranchi, Bokaro, Lohardagga were partly affected. East Singhbhum (Jamshedpur), West Singhbhum(Chaibasa),Dumka, Deoghar, Godda and Sahebganj disticts were free of these activities. Later four new districts namely Seraikela-Kharsawan, Latehar, Jamtara and Pakur were created in April 2001. Then the districts of Khunti and Ramgarh were created as the newest districts in September 2007.

Palamu

Palamu district was created in the year 1892. Migration from different parts of Bihar also made people settle here. With passage of time, feudalism characterised the place, gap between haves and the have nots developed when Rajputs and Bhumihar Zamindars started exploiting the subordinate classes. Atrosities against weaker sections, bonded labour, and sexual exploitations against poor sections gave rise to Naxal incidences in the region since 1987-88. By the time Jharkhand was created naxalism had spread its tentacles from Palamu to Chatra,Hazaribagh,Dhanbad and its adjoining areas. According to some evidences, the Naxalbari uprising also had influenced the adjoining area of Jamshedpur. Such evidences show that the comrades of Cheru Mazumdar had entered the remote areas of Jamshedpur, had tried to spread their ideologies and establish their bases. Naxal activists were arrested by Jamshedpur police, after a massive combing operation in the forest area, on the charges of armed attack on Jadugora police station in May, 1970. No evidence of further Naxal incidence exist till the period of creation of Jharkhand in this area. It was also because of arrest of Charu Majumdar by Calcutta police on 16th July 1972 and then his death in Lal Bazar police lockup on 28th July; that the revolutionary struggle suffered serious debacle as CPI(ML)'s central authority had collapsed.

Kolhan

Till the time of formation of Jharkhand, the Kolhan region that is the major portion of the old Singhbhum district comprising of Chaibasa, Jamshedpur and Saraikela was free from Naxal terror and was dominated by the Ho tribe. It is believed that immigrants came to the Singhbhum area from Manbhum during the 14th century or earlier. The Hos had a victory over the Bhuiyas (the then inhabitants) when they entered Singhbhum. In the latter half of the 18th century, the Hos fought wars against Rajas of Chotanagpur and

Mayurbhanj to retain independence. As far believed, the Muslims left them alone. Though the Muslims and the Marathas could have strong holds in the area due to their active holds in the surrounding areas, they didn't venture into the area. In 1765, the British East India Company overtook the Chotanagpur area as a part of Bihar, Bengal and Orissa. In 1767, the Raja of Singhbhum asked the Britishers resident at Midnapore for protection. But it was only after 1820, that he acknowledged himself as a feudatory to the Britishers. The Hos against it took part in the revolt of 1831-1833 together with the Mundas. The immediate cause for the 1831-32 uprising was the oppression of the Adivasis by the non Adivasi thekedars or the contractors. The Oraon tribes also joined the Hos and Mundas, houses of landlords, dikku (non adivasis or outsiders) were burnt, many people died. All such violence forced the Britishers to recognize the subjugation of the Hos. The uprisings were suppressed by the troops under Captain Wilkinson and Colonel Richard till 1836. All headmen were made to surrender within 3 months. Again in 1857, a revolt rose, was initiated by Raja of Porahat and was joined by much of the Hos. These disturbances were put to end by British troops by 1859. The customary laws of Mankis and Mundas were legalised during the British regime. They had been awarded administrative, judicial and other rights since long back in 1837. The Kolhan-Porahat region was divided into various peers and sub peers for administrative purposes by the Englishmen. Some of the duties of the policemen such as the general and collection of land revenues were also granted to the Mankis and Mundas. Powers had been granted to them such that the Mankis were made the chief police officers and the Mundas were made subordinates; they could apprehend offenders of any nature. The Resettlement of Kolhan Government Estate in l897 defined in detail the powers and functions of the Manki and Munda system and collection of land revenue. "The Munda is the village headman, and every village in the Kolhan has a Munda. He was responsible for the payment of the full rent of his village to Government less the commission due to the Manki, Tehsildar and himself. He received 16 per cent of the gross rent and 10 per cent goes to Manki and 2 per cent to the Tehsildar. The Manki is the headman over a group of villages, and is usually the Munda of the village in which he lives."

However the system weakened after independence in the area. The Winkinson's rule of protection of tribal rights also lost its respect in the state. The Manki Munda system strengthend in Jharkhand, after its formation and their power were recognised. Mundas being recognised as the village chiefmen had such powers that the arrests in the area couldn't be done without their help and association.

With the formation of the new state of Jharkhand, strives were also made by the Maoist groups to have their bases in the new areas. Such efforts were being made by the CPI (M), which was trying to make a corridor for its movement from West Bengal to Jamshedpur to Taboghati in Chaibasa to Saranda forest via Manoharpur and from saranda to the jungles of Orissa and in the areas of Chattisgarh. CPI(M) dastas could make a corridor through dense forest areas from West-Bengal to Jamshedpur-Chandil-Tamar-Arki to Khunti. But they were not able to move further through Bandgaon-Tabo-Manoharpur-Thalkobad and Saranda of the Chaibasa district. The reasons had been language problem, tough and hostile attitude of the Mundas and Hos of the area towards outsiders, and again the Manki Munda system. Retired IPS officer, Mr. Bimal Kishore Sinha had been the first Supretendent of Police for the area of West Singhbhum, he writes from his experience in his article "Naxalism in Jharkhand". Through his keen job and sources, he could contribute lot in understanding the situations. Together with the then Deputy Commissioner, Rajeev Arun Ekka, he realised the importance of the Manki Munda system in countering Naxalism from spreading its wings in the area. Thus they together tried to convince the Chiefminister Babu

Lal Marandi and the then Welfare minister Arjun Munda to accord legal recognision to the Manki Munda system. Dispite of lack of followed implementation measures, they themselves started carrying out measures to strengthen the system. In order to do so, regular meetings of the Mundas were started in every police station. Mundas thus were being encouraged to help more in countering Naxalism, they started giving information of Naxal activities in the area to the police and also built up resistant groups against any infilteration of suspected outsiders.

Mr. B.K.Sinha further writes about an intelligence of a Maoist group which already had establish its training camp in the forest of Sundergarh district of Orissa on the borders of Saranda. But the Sundergarh district police as well as the Orissa police headquartes refused to accept this intelligence as true. A small group of naxal leaders from AndhraPradesh and West-Bengal surveyed the forest area from Bandgaon to Saranda. They earmarked the Churches and Mission schools and started interacting with the teachers and students and through them tried to spread their ideology and gain support for food and shelter. They were indulged in this by sending an armed dasta of 30 activists. For the first time an armed dasta of MCC was observed in this area in 2000. The informations by the Mundas of the area initiated an encounter between the police and armed dasta of extremists in village Bitkalsoy under Manoharpur Police Station of this district which comes under Saranda forest area. Ishwar Mahto, a naxalite was killed and the earlier looted SLR by them from CRPF was retained.

The importance of the Mundas' association with the police comes here, that when the system's tactic of countering naxal insurgencies was no more felt important, the area became exposed to Naxal terror. Extremist had already announced to take revenge of the killing of Ishwar Mahto. They established training centres in Saranda and adjoining Sundergarh of Orissa and ultimately successed in their plan and ambushed the police party. 14 policemen and other personnel were killed and 30 regular weapons were also looted by them. The extremist groups successfully then established their hold together with training camps in this area. Acts of killing of policemen, attacks on police establishments, looting of weapons continued. Such was the attack on Bara Jamda police on 31st March 2004. Again 29 police personells were killed and more than 30 regular weapons were looted in a counter insurgency on 7th July 2004 near village Baliba under Gua police station of the district. The extremists by this time succeeded in establishing their authority in almost entire region of Saranda and formed the so desired Corridor from West-Bengal to Orissa and Chattisgarh via Saranda forest of Chaibasa.

Santhal Parganas

During the formation of Jharkhand, all regions were not naxal affected. Such also were the 6 districts of the Santhal Parganas- Dumka,Deoghar,Godda,Jamtara,Sahebganj and Pakur. But within 5 years, the presence of extrimists and their terror began to be felt here too when hand written posters of CPI (Maoist) were recovered at some places in the month of December-2005, January-2006 and April-2007. Dumpers of coal mines were put to blaze in Pakur. On 26 April 2008 three police personnel, including Officer-in-Charge Samsad Ansari, besides a Naxalite and a villager were killed in an encounter in Dumka district. This had taken place in a jungle located between Makropahari and Pokhria under Sikaripara police station. On 6th December, 2008, the Jharkhand Police opened fire on a procession of tribals, numbering between eight to ten thousands, 3 kilometres from Kathikund in Dumka district. The tribals were protesting against the setting up of a 1000 MW coal based power plant in Aamgachhi-Pokhariya villages of the area as well as against the earlier arrest of their colleagues. One tribal Lakhiram Tudu was killed, 7 suffered bullet injuries. The district administration and the government branded the organisations leading the protests, Jharkhand Ulgulan Manch and Jharkhand Hulgulan Mahila Manch as Maoists.

(*Source:* "Naxalism in Jharkhand"- by IPS [Retd.] Bimal Kishore Sinha)

Chapter – VI

A Present Day Scenario: Nexus with Corporate and Levy Extraction

According to the Union Home Minister, without cleansing Maoist insurgencies, development in the affected areas won't be possible. The statement was given by him before launching the Operation Green Hunt in November 2009. But his statement again on 1st April 2010, "Unless the State is able to provide them better security they will have to pay these rents to protect their investments", somehow justifies the extortion money paid by the corporate. According to the honest argument, If the corporate houses are indeed paying rent, they are abetting terrorism as provided under the Unlawful Activities Prevention Act, with the sanction of none other than the Home Minister. The villagers in situations when are forced to support the naxals at the gun point, are harassed by the police officials and often claimed to be supporters of Maoists. India obviously applies the anti-terrorism Act differently! Across the Naxalite affected areas covering approximately 40,000 square kilometers, many corporate houses are comfortably running their projects while the State has virtually lost its control.

"Corporate and the Maoists Nexus: a Case Study in Jharkhand", by Gladson Dungdung, presents a case study in Latehar, on the issue. The district of Latehar is known for its natural beauty forests and forest products. The district is rich in mineral deposits with coal, bauxite, laterite, dolomite, graphite, granite, quartz, fireclay and feldspar. Around 45.17 per cent of the population is of the tribal people. This Adivasi population has been facing economic crisis due to alienation from the natural resources, exploitation of the natural resources and climate change.

Latehar often suffer with Bands (shut downs), under the grip of the CPI (Maoists). Administration at such times becomes helpless in running even the district headquarters. The administration claims that the roads in pathetic conditions cannot be constructed due the fear of the CPI (Maoist). Also the development projects could not be initiated or are in very slow pace. Schools and health centers are also not run properly. But the ironical matter is that the corporate houses like Abhijeet Group, Essar Power and Hindalco have been running their projects smoothly in the district. The Corporate Power Limited (CPL), a unit of Kolkata based corporate house the Abhijeet Infrastructure Pvt. Ltd had been building up an independent thermal power plant at Chakla village, which comes under Chandwa block of Latehar district in Jharkhand since January 2008. The CPL signed an MoU with the Jharkhand government in 2007 for establishing a 1215 megawatt independent thermal power plant at Chakla village under Chandwa block in Latehar district with an estimated investment of Rs. 6080 crore. The company had planned to start a 540-megawatt unit in the first phase and 675-megawatt in the second phase. The government had allotted captive coal block to the company at Chitarpur of Latehar district, The company could even acquire No Objection Certificate from the State Polution Control Board without any public hearing. The company bought '400 acres of agriculture land from the local landholders at the price of Rs. 60 thousand per acre, which was later increased to Rs. 80 thousand per acre. When the company faced more problems, it started paying Rs. 5 lakh per acres. The company also promised to give one job in every 2 acres land. The company had assigned another Kolkata based firm called Simplex Infrastructures Limited for its major infrastructure development works, which had employed 4000 people including some former Maoists. The major workforce was hired from West Bengal and Bihar. Though the company had promised to give job to the landowners but no one had been appointed in the plant till late.

The Maoists have attacked the plants of the corporate houses whenever they failed to pay extortion money. The Maoists had also attacked Abhijeet Group's power plant in April 2009 and killed 4 security guards when the company refused to pay the levy. According to the local villagers nearby, the company had paid huge amounts of money to the Maoists. The Maoists have blocked 21 road construction projects sanctioned under the Pradhan Mantri Gram Sadak Yojana, when the contractors denied paying them levy.

The Intelligence Bureau officials alleged that Jharkhand based corporate houses like 'Rungta Mines, Usha Martin, Torian Iron & Steel have paid Rs.2.5 million each to the Maoists in 2007-08. Similarly, the Birla Boxite Company based in Palamu district paid Rs.8 million and Balumath (Latehar) based company Tetaria Mines paid Rs. 2 lakh to the Maoists in 2007-08. The list of the contractors paying huge amount of money every year to the Maoists for the construction of roads, bridges and government buildings is long. The CEO of Abhijit Group, Mr Arun Kumar Gupta stated that "Our ideology of providing development among the underprivileged perhaps matches the Maoists' ideology. That's why they are not disturbing our project".

The Jharkhand police have also been indulged in profit making from the existence of naxal belts. According to the Accountant General of Jharkhand (2006-2007 and

2007-2008), the then 'Director General of Police Vishnu Dayal Ram and the Additional Director General of Police Rajiv Kumar had withdrawn Rs 8 crore from the secret service fund and did not submit statements of expenditure. Moreover, a police informer 'Sanichar Pandit was asked to sign in vouchers as Amitabh Bachchan and was paid merely Rs 10,000 whereas Rs. 21 lakh was released in his name for providing information to the police regarding the Maoists. Often the government officials, teachers and health workers abstain from their duties blaming the Maoists but enjoy the full salary and other benefits. The contractors swallow the full amount of money sanctioned for the construction of roads, bridges and government buildings. The activities only have mentions on paper.

According to the secret service reports of the government of India, the iron ore, mines and crusher units of Jharkhand contribute Rs.500 crore to the Maoists. The illegal acts of the corporate are being supported by the government, the corporate which indeed is empowering the illegal existence of Maoists. Obviously, the links of the corporate and Maoists are not unknown to the government. In midst of all this, only the common men are the sufferers.

The amount of levy extracted by the Maoists is increasing and touching heights with passage of time. Just after the formation of the new state of Jharkhand during Chiefministership of Babu Lal Marandi, when the development works were not being allowed in the affected areas, to tackle with situations, 10 per cent of the estimates were decided to be lent to the Maoists. But the greed of these groups *increased* to extends such that now they demand 10 per cent from the government, and other 10 per cent from agencies or firms directly in concern, making total of 20 per cent. Due to differences in ideologies, the maoist groups have got split into squads Like the TSPC (Tritiya Sammelan Prastuti Committee), JPC (Jharkhand Prastuti Committee), JLT (Jharkhand Liberation Tigers), SJMM

(Sangharsh Jan Mukti Morcha), and SPM(Sashastra People's Morcha). The victims in all case are the common people. Though the splits have been on ideological differences, it seems that this fractional group has emerged only for the purpose of levy collections. The rich forest reserves with Kendu leaves, coal and minerals has made Jharkhand a grazing ground for easy collection of Levy money. Rs. 23.06 lakhs was recovered in 2008 alone, by the Jharkhand police. "Naxalism, which started off as a people's movement, has now become a nearly Rs 1500 crore organised extortion business in the form of 'levy'." Instead of using the huge extracted amounts for the running of the movement by the various splinter groups, it is usually made for maintenance of luxurious lifestyles for the masters. The total amount runs in several hundred crores every year. Other than the contractors, levy is also paid by the big industrial houses, also the nationally reputed ones. The naxal groups apart from the levy also indulge in kidnapping, looting and narcotics trade, which results in around Rs 300 crore as annual income from the state. The groups in this sense are not much different than other criminal gangs. The security forces feel that a conservative estimate of income generated in form of collections from the seven most Naxal-infested states—Jharkhand, Chhattisgarh,Andhra Pradesh, Orissa, Bihar,West Bengal and Maharashtra amounts to nearly 1,500 crores. A card even had been recovered from naxals showing the exact amount to be extracted from the contractors, landowners, and petrol pump owners. It usually ranges from 10 per cent of the project cost for those making unpaved roads to five per cent for small bridges and others. The amount is going on increase with time and no control over the extraction business. Besides the fixed levy, the left-wing extremists groups also demand money from industries functioning in the areas (as and when they need) and even issue receipts for the same. The People's Liberation Front of India, earlier known as Jharkhand Liberation Tigers, is mostly made up of criminals. According to CRPF DIG, Alok

Raj, it is not just the Naxals who approach contractors for money but in some cases even the contractors approach the Naxals with money. Director General of Police (Jharkhand) V D Ram said “In certain incidents, contractors have themselves approached the Naxals to blow up the roads built by them because they had used inferior material at first place. As the roads are blown away, no quality inspection takes place”. According to officials, the amount generated in the form of levy usually goes into a luxurious life style of Naxal chiefs. Though, they forcibly recruit children in their cadre, their own kids study in good public schools. The Naxals also encourage local villagers to undertake opium cultivation, just like insurgents in North-East states.

(*Source:* “Naxalism in Jharkhand; and

Corporate and the Maoists nexus - Asian Centre for Human Rights

www.achrweb.org/ihrrq/issue 1 /corporate.html)

Operation Green Hunt

CHAPTER – VII

COUNTER NAXAL TRENDS

After the formation of the new state of Jharkhand, Babu Lal Marandi had been the first Chief Minister. Under his ministership, many counter naxal policies were framed. The surrender policy formulated was much attractive, to have the Maoists surrender and for them to join the main stream. Babu Lal Marandi was the only Chief Minister who had the belief that the only cause for naxalism is not the poverty and underdevelopment in the state. According to him there lies the difference in politics through votes(what the political leaders do) and the political stream of the Maoists, that "Power is followed by the barrel of the gun." Babu Lal Marandi openly advocated against naxalism in the state and had to pay heavy price when his son was killed in naxal attack and he himself became the target of CPI (M). Sibu Soren as Chief Minister asked the Naxal Leaders of Jharkhand-Bihar-North Chattisgarh Area Committee to refrain from the path of violence and invited them to come over ground and have negotiations with the government. In 2004, a seminar was held on Left Wing Extremism at Counter Insurgency & Jungle Warfare School, Virengete, Mizoram. On the concluding day the then Chief Minister of Mizoram, Mr. Lal Thanhawla was the Chief Guest. He has been a militant turned politician. In the Mizo National Front (MNF) he had held the posts of assistant home secretary and Acting Foreign Secretary in the underground 'government in exile'. As Chief Guest his concluding speech was that both negotiation and police action should go simultaneously to control extremism.

Even the Supreme Court's Bench of Honb'le Judges B.Sudershan Reddy and Swatantra Singh Nijjar, while hearing the case related to so called killing of Dantewara (Chattisgarh) adivasis by the police, had remarked on 16th February,2010, that Naxalism is not a political problem nor it can only be controlled with police actions, it is linked with the problems of development. Adivasis and other under privileged people of the society can be diverted from joining the path of naxalism only by bringing them in the mainstream taking lead for their rehabilitation, education and livelihood.

(*Source:* "Naxalism in Jharkhand")

"Armed Communist insurgency is something that the nascent Indian nation-State—of which Sardar Patel was the home minister—confronted in Telangana even as the Constituent Assembly was debating the architecture of our Republican democracy founded on adult suffrage and positive discrimination in favor of scheduled castes and scheduled tribes." The phenomenon of Naxal violence has been studied by official committees from time to time. On initiation of Mrs. Indira Gandhi during her Prime Ministership, a team was sent headed by the-then member-secretary of the Planning Commission to conduct field-level studies of Naxal-affected areas in Bihar and Andhra Pradesh and recommend solutions, both for the Centre and the States to adopt. Amongst the recommendations was that urgent and long-festering socio-economic concerns of the weaker sections of society must be addressed meaningfully if the influence of Naxal groups is to be countered effectively.

(*Source:* "The tribal cause is a mask to further the Naxal agenda strategicstudyindia. blogspot.com/.../the-tribal-cause-is-mask-t...)o-further.ht

The two pronged strategy of dealing with the naxal problems, as per the Home Minister P. Chtambram's statements has been appropriate police action led by state governments in collaboration with central forces together with the development works in the affected areas to deal with the Maoist rebellion. This two pronged strategy has been described as the "carrot and stick" approach by the author of "Analysis of the situation in 2012, of 11/6/13", the stick being here the Operation Green Hunt (OGH) and it's successors Operation Haka etc, with the entry of the Indian Army in direct operations. The carrot had been various schemes as the Integrated Action Plan (IAP), Prime Minister's Rural Development Fellowship Scheme (PMRDFS) and other related schemes.

Operation Green Hunt had been a new phase in the old war. Appropriation of Avarna resources had been an old strategy; the population itself had retreated deeper into the forests and interior regions, under the onslaught of the Savarna rule. The indigenous population got confined into these areas, the dominance of Savamas reduced their conditions to that of annihilation of their way of life and transfer of all their lands, rivers, forests into the hands of corporations owned by puppet Savarna individuals and their foreign masters. With its "Search and Combing" operations, the Operation Green Hunt by 2009 was being carried out in maoist influenced districts of central India. By November 2009, the progress of the Operation Green Hunt was being recorded by the press and media, this prompted Home Minister P. Chitambram to term the operation a "Media Invention", The mentions of Green Hunt since then have scrupulously been avoided by the security apparatus. All the efforts resulting in the operation had been initiated in 2006 after Prime Minister's declaration of Naxal terror as the biggest threat to India,; and its further exaggerated fumes. To avoid any slack of pace of mobilisation and any let down in the guard of administration, the threat of maoist need to be raised at regular intervals. The deployment of OGH had also been influenced by the Sri Lankan military's total annihilation of the Tamil Tigers in Eelam War IV which ended in May 2009. The greatest element of influence was that the tiny island nation of Sri Lanka could rout the LTTE (A non-state actor which had its own navy, air force and was building its own submarines. India then has the world's largest standing volunteer army. Together with the grid system which had been successful in Sri Lanka, need for an additional force like the Rashtriya Rifles (which could make the grid system successful in Jammu Kashmir) had been felt for countering naxalism, especially in Chattisgarh, Jharkhand and Maharashtra. In 2009, an attempt was made to induct the Rashtriya Rifles into anti-naxal operations but the Army was reluctant to redeploy them for various reasons.

There have been large scale recruitment and deployment of tribal personnel as a part of the Operation Green Hunt. The situations have not been much different from that during the British rule when the tribals loyal to Britishers were made to counter the tribal revolutionaries against the rule. It can be said that Salwa Judum was merely a 21st century manifestation of an 18th century idea. Both the Indian Army and various state governments intend to recruit Avarna's and engage them in a fratricidal war. Operation green hunt was to focus on 78 IAP districts spread across 9 states identified by the government of India. The aim of Operation Green Hunt had been to clear these areas off Maoists and then launch development activities. One key strategy of OGH remained to first break the contiguous ring and then box the Maoists into areas isolating them from their comrades in other districts. This was supposed to lead to the fragmentation of the Maoist controlled areas and cause complications to the Maoist leadership in the long run. Planning and construction of roads under the Pradhan Mantri Gram Sadak Yojna (PMGSY) in strategic locations to fragment the ring of fire and provide support to security forces had also been the part. OGH aimed to inflict heavy losses and increase the body count of Maoists substantially.

The Intelligence Bureau has been complementing the effort by going after top Maoist leaders in urban areas and those leaders who...venture out of the jungle bases. The role of the army had been such that an assessment had been made for *required* troops, trainings had already been provided too much in the acquired *training* bases and these troops then indulged themselves in counter naxal insurgencies. Recruitment of IPS officers from the army had been included in the strategy with an intension of then putting them in Operation *Green* Hunt.

There also had been plans of having contributions of the air force for the operations. A separate Air-Wing for Anti-Maoist operations had been in the plans. In 2009, a 1,300-m airstrip was constructed in the Counter Terrorism and Jungle Warfare College Campus.

According to the Indian government, getting the logistics of troop deployment right and ensuring the supply chain functions could play an important role in the success of the campaign. While the Maoists live of land and have support from the local population, the Paramilitary has to ensure a regular supply of food and rations from a hostile population and access to medical facilities in case of injuries.

The government of India already was aware that the merger of PWG and MCCI would strengthen the maoist hold and activities in the respective area. Since 2007/08 the government began making serious efforts in augmenting the capabilities of the security forces. This had been reflective in the report released by the Ministry of Home Affairs in December 2011.

3 Year Report on Major tasks accomplished by Ministry of Home Affairs

Extract from the Report

"Left Wing Extremism : LWE

The following interventions have been made to contain the growth of Naxalite movement in the country:

CPI (Maoist) included in the Schedule to UA(P)A and declared terrorist organisation.

5 Polit bureau members and 7 other Central Committee members of CPI (Maoist) in custody.

Number of CAPF battalions deployed in LWE affected States increased from 37 in 2008 to 73 in Nov 2011. In addition, 10 cobra battalions also deployed.

Capacity building of State police forces in 9 LWE affected States through enhanced allotment in 2011-12 under Security Related Expenditure Scheme (SRE) (Rs.598 cr) and Scheme for Special Infrastructure (SIS) (Rs.362 cr).

Focused development of 60 Tribal and backward LWE affected districts in 9 LWE affected States through Integrated Action Plan (IAP). 63,416 projects sanctioned, of which 26,593 completed, incurring an expenditure of Rs. 1,391 cr till Nov 2011.

Monitoring of flagship and other development schemes in LWE affected districts by the Planning Commission.

A road requirement plan (RRP-1) for 5565 km in LWE affected areas at a cost of Rs. 7,300 cr approved by CCEA in Feb 2009.

Construction/strengthening of 400 fortified police stations at a cost of Rs.2 Cr per police station approved on 20 June 2010."

The ground reality however has been different from the above initiatives on paper.

"Analysis Of the Situation in 2012, Of 11/6/13" states that Despite many claims of the cumulative 'improvement' in the capacities of central and State Security Forces (SFs), the state's vulnerabilities remained largely unaddressed.

The Union Ministry of Home Affairs' (UMHA) November 30, 2011, claimed that the police-population ratio had been raised to 176 per 100,000, while according to the National Crime Records Bureau figure of 133 per 100,000 as on December 31, 2010 becomes clear. UMHA's claims of "significant measures taken to strengthen the Indian Police Service" (IPS) remain something of a smokescreen, since existing deficits in the Service will take decades to fill, even with dramatically accelerated intakes. UMHA also claims that "Number of CAPF (Central Armed Police Force) battalions deployed in LWE (Left Wing Extremist) affected States increased from 37 in 2008 to 73 in November 2011. This has roughly been the level of deployment, since the disastrous 'massive and coordinated operations' were launched by the Centre in end-2009. But during incidences like the Chintalnad massacre of April 2010, the state police Special Forces were found to have frozen in a passive defensive posture. Offensive operations against the Maoist have now become more and more the exception among demoralised SF contingents. According to one devastating disclosure, the UMHA conceded that as many as 46,000 officers and personnel took voluntary retirement from the CAPF between 2007 and September 2011, while another 5,220 officers and personnel resigned from service over the same period. 461 suicides and 64 instances of fratricides were also recorded. Worse, UMHA noted that the rate of increase of cases of resignation in the CRPF and Border at more than 70 per cent in 2011, over 2010. The principal Maoist affected States, Odisha, Jharkhand, West Bengaj and Bihar suffer from equal and endemic deficiencies in their security structures, as well as from both ambivalence and infirmity in their political leaderships. Then there have been anomalies directing Operation Green Hunt that supposedly resulted in the murder or suicide of the SP- Rahul Sharma. It has been disheartening that a Superintendent of Police had to commit suicide to get his point across, an issue that can certainly influence the morale and motivation of his minions down the order. Also when IPS officers over-looking Anti-Maoist operations regularly succumb to heart attacks it hardly evokes confidence in the ability of the police force. Such had been the scenario in the initiative phase of the operation, and from a normal point of view till the concerns are not strongly paid attention; the conditions can be worse further. Though the broad general trend among the security forces seems to be an increase in co-operation, capacity building, training and coordination but they are still far from finding their mojo.

Together with the infliction of heavy casualties on the maoist squads through the counter programs like OGH (stick), others like the Integrated Action Plan and PMRDF have been in plans to seek to prevent fresh recruitment to the Maoist fold by providing incentives, alternate sources of livelihood to the local population. Alienating the support base of Maoists by providing civic amenities and financial benefits. Has been the only purpose of the IAP and PMRDF- prevent fresh blood from joining the Maoist fold and keep their attention diverted towards other illusions. Circulation of money from Delhi bank account to the IAP districts, bank accounts are initiated under IAP for development and expenditure. Jairam Ramesh had asked the Prime Minister for an additional allocation of Rs 35,000 Crore for the IAP districts over the *next* three years. This plan has been in operation for the last 2 years but the results have been sketchy and mixed. The number of IAP districts stood at 78, after more districts were added. The expansion of the IAP to districts that have only a marginal presence of Maoists shows that it is also being used as a preemptive measure.

Following presents an overview of IAP:-

Integrated Action Plan to Develop Tribal and backward Districts in LWE Areas

Introduction

At the time of presentation of the budget for the year

2010-11, the Government had announced its decision to introduce a special scheme to address the development of 33 Left Wing Extremism (LWE) affected districts. It was inter-alia, stated that the Planning Commission would prepare an Integrated Action Plan (IAP) for the affected areas and that adequate funds would be made available to support the action plan. The 33 districts (later expanded to 34) referred to in the Finance Minister's announcement were a sub-set of the 83 LWE affected districts identified by the Ministry of Home Affairs for coverage under its Security Related Expenditure (SRE) Scheme. This sub-set consisted of those districts where more than 20% of the Police Stations experienced some incidents of naxal violence. Subsequently, West Medinapur district of West Bengal was added to the list due to the situation prevailing there, taking the total to 35 districts.

Implementation of IAP

IAP was formulated as an additional central assistance scheme on 100 per cent grant basis in November 2010. To begin with, the Integrated Action Plan (IAP) for 60 tribal and backward districts was to be implemented with a block grant of Rs.25 crore and Rs.30 crore per district during 2010-11 and 2011-12 respectively for which the funds were to be placed at the disposal of the Committee headed by the District Collector and consisting of the Superintendent of Police of the district and the District Forest Officer. The district level committee will have flexibility to spend the amount for development schemes according to need, as assessed by it. The Committee would draw up a Plan consisting of concrete proposals for public infrastructure and services such as School Buildings, Anganwadi Centres, Primary Health Centers, Drinking Water Supply, Village Roads, Electric Lights in public places such as PHCs and Schools etc. The concerned Development Commissioner/ equivalent officer in charge of development in the State shall be responsible for scrutiny of expenditure and monitoring of

IAP. The Planning Commission will undertake macro level monitoring of the scheme and implementation of the scheme will be reviewed and suitable decisions taken on the modalities for implementation of the scheme as a part of the 12th Five Year Plan.

The salient features of the guidelines are:

(i) The district level committee should draw up a plan consisting of concrete proposals for public infrastructure and services such as school buildings, Anganwadi centres, Drinking Water supply, Village Roads, electric lights in public places such as PHCs and schools etc. The schemes so selected should show results in the short term.

(ii) A suitable form of consultation is to be ensured with the local Members of Parliament on the schemes to be taken up the under the IAP.

(iii) The expenditure on the projects should be over and above the expenditure being incurred for the regular State/Centra!/Centra!!y Sponsored Schemes. The district level committee should ensure that there is no duplication of expenditure on the same project.

(iv) The State Government will release the funds directly into the bank account opened for this purpose by the District Collector or District Magistrate. The State Government will ensure that funds are transferred to this bank account within 15 days of the release of the funds to the Consolidated Fund of the State Government failing which the State Government should transfer to the district penal interest at RBI rate.

Achievements turner IAP

The implementation of the scheme commenced in the year 2010-11 and Rs.25 crore per district i.e. total Rs. 1500 crore for the year 2010-11 was released in December, 2010. The districts immediately finalised the works to be taken up, completed the tender processes wherever required and the works on the ground commenced immediately in all the 60 districts. Currently, the implementation of IAP in the districts is in full swing. The total funds released so far for the year 2011-12 is Rs. 1090 crore and the total funds released so far since the commencement of the Scheme is Rs.2590 crore. Against the total amount of Rs 2590 crores released so far to the 9 States, the expenditure as on 27.12.2011 is Rs. 1468.83 crore i.e. 56.71 per cent of the funds released. Under the IAP, *so* far 62327 projects for an amount of Rs. 3230.02 crore have been taken up in the 9 States. These include construction of School Buildings/School Furniture, Anganwadi Centres, Drinking Water facilities, Rural roads, Panchyat Bhawan/Community Halls, Godowns/PDS shops, livelihood activities, skill development/trainings, minor irrigation works, electric lighting, health centres/facilities, Ashram Schools, construction of toilets, construction of multi-purpose chabutra, construction of passenger waiting hall, special coaching classes for students, construction of ANM centres, development of play grounds etc.

44.42 per cent of projects taken up so far have been completed i.e., 27687 projects have been completed so far.

The given table shows the physical progresses as on 27th Dec, 2011.

State	*Completed projects*	*Sanctioned projects*
Andhra Pradesh	702	1140
Bihar	2367	12889
Chhattisgarh 6115	14718	
Jharkhand	5621	11769
Madhya Pradesh	1446	5352
Maharashtra	2667	4398
Orissa	6829	15087
Uttar Pradesh	1337	1548
West Bengal	303	1272

The Planning Commission during the formulation of the scheme also considered that the projects should not only be articulated for severely LWE affected districts, but to other tribal and backward districts too. Thus for identification of districts under the scheme, the following criteria was adopted.

(a) Whether the district is included in the list of 83 SRE districts identified by the Ministry of Home Affairs;
(b) Whether the tribal population exceeds 25 per cent;
(c) Whether the forest area exceeds 30 per cent;
(d) Whether the poverty ratio in the district exceeds 50 per cent; and
(e) Whether the district is covered under the Backward Regions Grant Fund (BRGF).

Districts meeting four of the above-mentioned five criteria and forming a contiguous block were selected for coverage under the proposed scheme. Thus, with these criteria, a total of 60 districts were selected for coverage under the scheme.

The Development Commissioner of the State/equivalent officer in charge of development in the State is responsible for scrutiny of expenditure and monitoring of the IAP in the State. In order to facilitate the monitoring, the States are required to send district-wise monthly progress reports in the prescribed format and also upload the information on the Management Information System(MIS) along with photographs of the works. Regular monitoring of the IAP is being carried out by the Member-Secretary, Planning Commission through video conferences with the District Collectors/District Magistrates and Development Commissioner of the States concerned.

The Ministry of Home Affairs has also constituted an Empowered Group of Officers with Member-Secretary, Planning Commission as its Chairperson. The Empowered Group, interalia, has overriding powers to modify existing norms/guidelines on implementation of various development programmes and flagship schemes in consultation with the Ministries/Departments concerned.

The Integrated Action Plan was successful and the scheme had a good response in the manner that number of requests had been received from the Chief Ministers, Members of Parliament and State Governments for inclusion of more districts under the IAP.

Jairam Ramesh, the Union Rural Development Minister on Prime Minister's Rural Development Fellowship Scheme (PMRDFS); "The aim of the unique scheme is simple. "If the Maoists attract youth through their ideology, then the government has to counter that in a similar way."

PMRDFs is to function basically as development facilitators, assisting the Collector and his/her colleagues by actively pursuing a district programming approach that follows three key strategies given below:

Strengthen the district resource base for programming by finding ways of resourcing all the planned activities and rational budgeting.

Establish or strengthen systems by exploring alternative ways of delivering services to reach the most deprived communities.

Trigger processes which would support the changes that have been envisioned in this approach (e.g. village planning).

Along with IAP and PMRDF's, there are various other schemes like Job Schemes etc which have been rolled out and many more which are components of the IAP and currently in stealth mode.

The key to winning any battle is knowing what your opponent is going to do before he does."

The government has a greater capacity and staying power than the Maoists and can take greater losses and incur a higher expenditure over a sustained period. India has an unemployment rate of 7-10 per cent. Which means there are an estimated 70-100 million idle minds and hands in this country at any point of time. It is very easy for the government to train some of these and put guns in their hands, unlike the Maoists who have to operate, recruit and train under severe constraints. 'The Avarna's under the leadership of the Maoists will then have to face the question of whether they will make their stand militarily or whether they can counter the offensive through non-military means." (*Source:* Analysis of the situation in 2012 | Naxalite Maoist India naxalrevolution.blogspot.com/2012/04/analysis-of-situation-in-2012.html)

The Sarranda forests of West Singhbhum had been reclaimed from naxal dominance in 2011, but started witnessing attacks again from 2012. Development works had been introduced under the Saranda Action Plan (SAP). Just a month after work started on road construction under the Pradhan Mantri Gram Sadak Yojana (PMGSY) as part of the SAP, Maoists set ablaze four dumpers and two earth movers (Josephy Cyril Bamford Ltd) in Ushariya village of Digha Panchayat in West Singhbhum District. Union Rural Development Minister Jairam Ramesh had been personally monitoring implementation of SAP, and had already made at least four visits to Saranda to monitor the implementation of the development plan. Despite this, on September 12, 2012, at Digha, Ramesh apologized to the people for the tardy pace of development work due to the "Naxal activities".

Before 'Operation Anaconda IT, SFs had conducted some large cordon and search operations in the State. 'Operation Octopus', launched in April in Latehar District; 'Operation Thunder' in Jhumra hills in Bokaro District in May; Operation 'Rain Storm' in Garhwa District in July-end; and 'Operation Marangdeo' on the Jharkhand-Chhattisgarh borders in August, all in 2012. However, the operational efficiency of such large scale campaigns is open to debate.

Jharkhand's Police Population ratio (Policemen per 100,000 populations) was 167 as on December 31, 2011, well above the national average of 137, but substantially below the level needed to deal with the State's complex problems of law and order administration and security. 18 battalions of CRPF had also been deployed in the State, and another five battalions were likely to be added shortly, in view of the latest encounter at Latehar.

Compounding Jharkhand's fraught security situation is political instability. There is a need for a better alignment of the Centre's and State's anti-Maoist orientation. However, given the results of large-scale area domination exercises, dramatic improvements are unlikely,unless there is a dramatic improvement in intelligence capabilities, and the escalation of targeted, intelligence led special operations.

(*Source:* "Maoist: Jharkhand Assessment 2013 - South Asia Terrorism Portal" www.satp.org/satporgtp/countries/ india/.../Assessment/...ZJharkhand.htm)

THE SPREADING
NAXALITE THREAT

CHAPTER – VIII

NAXALISM IN JHARKHAND: VIOLATION OF HUMAN RIGHTS

The ugly truth is that, the naxal terror is not only a problem in itself, but has many consequential and related aspects. Some case studies and reports from fact finding teams in and around some pockets can be helpful in highlighting this perspective.

Report on the Massacre in Baruhatu

On 19th November, 2010, news of brutal killing of 4 villagers of Baruhatu under Bundu block of Ranchi district, flashed on the news channels and got published in the news papers. After the incident, the villagers called for a bandh under the leadership of Special Police Officers, to protest the killings. They also demanded for protection of Special Police Officers and compensation to the bereaved families as well.

The Baruhatu village lies at 5 kilometres west of the block head office. The team denoted 5000 people reciding in the village from about 1200 families.

In around 60' clock in the evening, when it was drizzling, gun shots were heard. Four people were murdered, Pradeep

Singh Munda, his 6 years old daughter Manisha Kumari, Sanjay Mahto and Sonaram Munda. Pradeep's 10 years old daughter, Reshmi Kumari was also hit by bullet in her leg. The incidence took place in Pradeep's house in Manki Tola. The four persons were killed by two men equipped with firearms, they fled the sceen after firing. The report of murder was made by the villagers to the police, which arrived after one and half hours, dispite that the police camp was only 200 to 250 metres away from the spot. The dead bodies were sent for post mortem and the young injured girl was sent to RIMS for treatment. Lakhimuni Devi, Pradeep's wife while narrating the incidence told that at time of the incidence, the three killed men were chatting together in the room and Pradeep's daughter was on her father's lap. Pradeep's other daughters were also in the room.

Pradeep had been working in behalf of police with other youths of the locality. His wife agreed that her husband had been murdered by the Maoists only. Earlier, he used to work for the Maoists, after quitting, he had been working as an SPO (special police officer), for the police and used to provide them information. All the men, Pradeep and his friends were police informers and used to Sleep in police camps at night. Pradeep had also been given a country made gun which he used to bring to his home sometimes. He had 3 acres of land which was the main source of livelihood for the family.

Together with the conversations with these people, the fact finding team also had conversations with two other youths, Trilok Pahan (18 years) and the other Umakant Patar (17 years). Both of them came to join in the last rites of the deceased. Both lived in Manki Tola. All these people, the two boys and the three deceased men had been working together as spies for the police. There work was to inform police about people coming into the village, people going where, who is linked with the Maoists, etc. They used to spend most of the time with the police team and wandering around with them in the locality. The five had been working as spies since last 6 months from the incidence. They had been promised for payment of rupees 300 per month for the work, but had not been payed the amount, were going to be paid recently as assured by the SSP. Umakant had studied up to matriculation. Before working as a police spy, he was a member of a Maoist squad. "I was arrested by the Tamar police, along with Sripati Munda in January 2009. They let me off after 15 days as I was underage, but sent Sripati Munda to jail. The day we got caught, we had gone to Tamar area to visit Deema Pahan, brother of Kundan Pahan." He said "The Maoist ideology is not right and that is the reason behind my leaving their party. After my arrest the Maoists didn't provide any financial assistance either to me or my family. Before joining them I used to run a shop for my bread and butter. By the time I left the party, everything was destroyed. I was looking for some means to meet my both ends need. Meanwhile the police contacted me and I turned to be a police informer. I'm working as a spy since six months. We are 16 boys who work for the police. Three boys are from other village and rest of them belong to our village. Maoists have killed 3 boys among the 16." The informers had been given just one double barrel gun, which could take in 0.315 cartridges. They had also been given 10 cartridges along with the gun, but they couldn't move out of the camp with that.

The fact finding team became aware of some facts through conversations with the villagers. According to the villagers, there was a police camp set up there in the local Rajkiya Madhya Vidyalaya since 2008. Initially the CRPF jawans used to stay there, and at that time JAP-1 jawans had set up camps there. After the incident a Battalion of JAGUAR had also been deployed in the camp. Around 300 local children had been registered in this school, but the school was being run in the Panchayat Bhavan owing to the stay of police jawans in the school. Since two months only two rooms were being used as class rooms, this situation further discouraged the children to come to school and their presence had become very less. Most of them grazed their cattle and did house hold work. Mid-day meal was not served in the school; even Anganvadi was not working properly. Most of the bore well hand pumps were out of order. Primary Health Centre, PHC building was severely damaged. The PHC was now being run in the Panchayat Bhavan. ANM nurse Pramila Kumari and Compounder Parmeshwar Munda seldom came to the PHC. No doctor had visited the PHC till then. People depended on the quacks for their medical needs. The village had been electrified in the year 1993, but the electric wires got theft in the year 1995. The village had not been electrified since then.

The situations were observed to be pathetic. Despite of the availability of a separate camp building for the police, the school building was being used by the police; only two rooms in the school were being utilised for studies. Out of the total number of students registered, only 100 were attending the classes. Though the Primary Health Centre was temporarily being run in the Panchayat Bhawan, the building was found closed on all days the team made visits. A heap of sign boards and notice boards related to NREGA and other schemes were found lying near the Panchayat Bhavan. As these boards were related to some schemes, they were supposed to be put at the work place. This showed that there was heavy irregularity in the implementation of NREGA schemes. There was total lack of safe drinking water in the village. There was no facility for irrigation. There was no provision for employment. Lack of opportunities of guidance to youths was resulting in youths joining maoist squads or being spies for the police. There was reign of terror in the village. The production of country liquor was on increase and the police jawans used to consume it a lot, openly. In this situation the villagers were producing more liquor for meager profits. More production was resulting in more consumption by the villagers.

The children in the village were put on household work. These all brought the economic, social activities and cultural activities at stake.

After the observations, the following recommendations were made by the Fact Finding Team.-

- There should be an impartial and high level investigation into the Baruhatu massacre.
- The police camp should be removed immediately from the school building. According to the supreme court orders)
- There should be immediate ban on the use of local youth as police spy and special police officers. (According to the supreme court orders)
- Some youth are kept in the police camp; a high level probe should be conducted in this matter. Stern action should be taken against the guilty police officers.
- Immediate and appropriate compensation be paid and a member of each of the bereaved families should be given government job as well.
- Security arrangement of the village should be rectified and also the police camp should be withdrawn from the village immediately.
- Government should ensure that the villagers and the rural youth get enough opportunities of employment.
- To confuse the youth and using them for personal gain by the police should immediately be stopped.
- The youth working for the police as S.P.O. since six months, on just the verbal assurance given by the senior police official, should be paid their dues immediately.
- The three youth killed in this gruesome incident, Pradeep Singh Munda, Sanjay Mahto and Sonaram Munda were working as SPO for the police. They were not employed through any proper recruitment process. They were working for the police on the verbal

assurance given by the Senior Police Officer. Some other youth are working day and night with the jawans of the police camp. The youth who died in this attack should be award the status of martyr by the police department. Equal amount of compensation and government job to the member of the family should be provided as it is provided in the case of martyrdom of police personnel.

(*Source:* Fact Finding Team's Report on the Massacre in Baruhatu Village Under Bundu Block)

Report on an Incidence in Ladi Village

The following is an investigative study made by the **Anti operation green hunt Citizen's Forum.**

Prime Minister Manmohan Singh in 2008, had termed Maoism as the biggest internal security threat to the country and a challenge for capital investment. Since then around 92,000 Sq. Km. area with a majority of tribal population was identified as "Red Corridor" or "Lalgarh". After this, a special police operation was started in the name of elimination of Maoists and it was named "Operation Green hunt". This operation faced huge opposition in Jharkhand and couldn't get started but on March 5th 2010 it was formally set in motion in Singhbhum District. It came to Latehar district at the same time.

The Fact Finding Team made a visit to Ladi village under Barwadih Block in Latehar district, Jharkhand. An incidence had taken place in Ladi village, which is located 60 KMs away from district headquarter Latehar, in the middle of the Jungle, on 27th April 2010; a Tribal Khairwar women was shot dead and one shepherd was wounded. According to the local police, the deaths were the result of an encounter between the police and the Maoists.

The encounter had taken place between the police and Maoists near the Ladi village in Barwadih Block. In around 7:30 in the evening, the police entered the village. Gunshots were heard. A few moments' later policemen encircled the house of Village Head Kameshwar Singh, shouting "come out of the house or else it will be burnt down." Hearing this, nervous family members of Kameshwar Singh came out of the house. Kameshwar Singh and his son Jairam Singh used to work as temporary staff in forest department and this being the reason they were not present at home. After hearing the policemen, Vishram Singh (18), younger son of Kameshwar Singh, came out opening the door. Policemen took hold of him and tied his hands to his back and pointed a gun at him. After pinning him down, one policeman asked vishram sing's sister-in-law Jacinta Devi whether anyone else was there inside the house. She replied "A shepherd, Puran Singh (62) is sleeping inside." She was told to wake him up and bring him outside. When she was coming out along with the Shepherd, policemen opened fire. A bullet hit her went inside her chest, she fell down and died. Policemen fired again, it hit Puran Singh's hand and he was wounded as well. Seeing the dead body, family members started crying. The Police told them to keep quiet or else everyone will be shot dead. They also accused saying- "you people provide food to the Maoists." Immediately after the incident, police took away the entire family including wounded Puran Singh and the dead body with them. They threatened the family that they should tell others that Jacinta Devi was killed in an encounter. They also asked not to take out any rallies.

The villagers didn't have any idea where the dead body was taken, so on April 28th 2010 they blocked the Mahuadanr-Daltonganj Main Road. After the post-mortem in Sadar Hospital Latehar, the police took Vishram Singh's signature on a blank paper and handed over the dead body to family members for the last rites. Vishram Singh hired a vehicle paying Rs. 4000/-and brought the body to the village. Barwadih CO. provided Rs. 10,000/- to them under the family benefit scheme. On April 30th 2010 relatives of the deceased and the villagers went to Barwadih police station to register a case against the murder of Jacinta Devi but Station-In-Charge Ratanlal Saha didn't register their case, he recorded the information in the diary instead and threatened them to go back.

After the protest by the villagers administration assured them of Rs. 3 lakh as compensation. One local journalist Manoj Vishwakarma (Hindustan) was mediating in this matter at the behest of the police. On May 14th 2010 Manoj Vishwakarma took Jairam Singh, the husband of the deceased to Barwadih Police Station where the Station In-charge Birendra Ram told Jairam Singh to put his signature on a blank paper in order to receive a cheque of Rs. 90,000/- when Jairam Singh refused to put his signature on the blank paper, Station In-charge sent him back empty handed.

After the brutal killing of Jacinta Devi her husband was not only left to struggle to find the means of livelihood but had to play the role of a mother too. His three young children, Amrita Kumari (5), Suchit Kumar (3) and vibha Kumari (1) (at that time), had lost their childhood and their future became uncertain.

Some facts were found by the team, after investigation:-

1. Inspection of the house of the deceased made it clear that there was only one door to enter in the house. A wall of the house had the marks of two bullets which were fired at the direction of the entry door. In case of an encounter bullets should have been shot from inner portion of the house aiming towards the door. After Jacinta Devi was killed, police entered and searched the house. If there were any Maoists inside the policemen would have caught them. Furthermore absence of any other door in the house ruled out any possibility of their escape. Inspection of place of incident, statements of relative of deceased, shepherd and villagers made it very clear that Jacinta Devi was not killed in an encounter but the police murdered her.

2. Police tried to put this incident as an encounter. For this reason the application submitted by the victim's family protesting the murder of Jacinta Devi, case was not registered and family of the deceased was being threatened continuously.
3. Earlier administration promised Rs. 3 lac as compensation but when deceased's husband Jairam Singh wanted to receive the compensation he was told that in order to get Rs 90,000 he will have to sign some blank papers first. This highlights the fact that Barwadih police wanted to misappropriate the compensation money.
4. After this incident villagers of Ladi were made to live in constant fear, police might come anytime and could torture anybody.
5. Puram Singh alias Baleshwar Singh, the shephered of Kameshwar Singh had become handicapped in the shooting incident. He was undergoing treatment in Sadar Hospital Latehar and was kept under the supervision of armed forces. Latehar civil surgeon Arun Tigga didn't know anything about Puran Singh.

The following recommendations were made by the Fact Finding Team:-

1. A high level judicial inquiry of this incident must be done.
2. A case of murder should be registered against the policemen involved in this killing and the hardest punishment be awarded to them.
3. Taking legal action against Station In-Charge becomes necessary for not registering a case about this murder.
4. Legal action must be taken against police officials who tried to misappropriate the compensation money.
5. Suspension and legal action should be taken against the Dy.S.P, who tried to white wash and hush up the incident, the then station-in-charge at the time of

incident Ratan Lal Saha and incumbent station incharge Birendra Ram.

6. Rs. 10 lacs as compensation be paid to the family of the deceased woman, Govt. job and free education to children. Rs. 5 lacs as compensation be given to the wounded shepherd Puran Singh.
7. Protection to the family of the deceased.
8. Basic amenities should be made available in the village.
9. Police atrocities on villagers must come to an immediate stop.
10. This is not an isolated event such incidents are taking place at a regular interval in Jharkhand. If we stop them then Operation Greenhunt- which is being conducted under the pretence of finishing off Maoism must come to an immediate halt.

(*Source:* Report of an investigative study made by the Anti operation green hunt Citizen's Forum)

Murder of Niyamat Ansari" a Case Study, And Developmental Perspectives

Neyamat Ansari was murdered on 2nd march 2011. The news spread and strives were being made to gain informations about the incidence. A close associate of Neyamat Ansari, Mr. James Herenj gave detailed information about the said incident. Social activists from various groups, journalists, human rights activists, members of MNREGA national council- Jean Drej and his associates reached Manika block under Latehar district from Delhi after the murder of Neyamat Ansari and sought information about this brutal incident.

On 5th march 2011 a vernacular Daily Newspaper reported that one of the accused of the murder has been arrested. On 7th march 2011 newspapers reported that a local Maoist squad has taken the responsibility for the murder of Neyamat Ansari. They put forth three reasons behind his murder:- Being a police informer; Wasting forests and forcibly acquiring forest land; Charges of embezzlement of funds and Taking bribes.

Noted intellectuals of the country condemned Neyamat Ansari's murder and they demanded an apology and explanation from Maoist central committee for this brutal murder and sought protection for Bhukhan Singh, an associate of Neyamat Ansari. The killing was also condemned by PUDR on 8th March with demand for handing of responsible Maoists It also asked for an apology from the Maoists and sought protection for Bhukhan Singh. Police and administration made serious allegations against Neyamat Ansari in local and National led Newspaper. Later, Indian Express apologized for publishing unverified reports. Local newspapers published the statement of Bhukhan Singh after the incident. He was under police protection and during this period while staying at the state capital Ranchi he gave his statement through a newspaper. This gruesome act was severely condemned by many (people) Organisations, Intellectuals and social activists.

Following is the summary of the videotaped statement of Bhukhan Singh and his family on 9th March, by the investigation team:-

In his statement he told about the initial days of his struggle with regard to his social activities. He raised doubts on the various aspects related to this incident:

- He started his struggle with a fight against the exploitation of villagers by the Forest Department. He continued his struggle and brought justice to the villagers.
- He protested against the loot in various schemes and funds. He constructed a check dam at a cost of Rs 4,75,000/- through "Pani Panchayat" and demonstrated the correct implementation of Govt. schemes. By doing this he put forward an example by providing laborers with lift and minimum wages.

- He also participated in the nationwide movement related to making of laws with regard to NREGA, Right to Information Act and Forest Rights Act. After the laws came into effect, he fought for their implementation on the ground level as well.
- Currently he is associated with Action Aid's project "Gram Swaraj" movement and NREGA information centre which is run by Jean Drej. He told that the honorarium meant for him and Neyamat Ansari has been stopped since October 2010 by the officials of the Organisation related to this movement. The officials allege that these two activists had taken part in Panchayat elections.
- When Jean Drej from NREGA Information Centre came to know about this he assured Neyamat and him to provide an honorarium of Rs. 3600/- per month.
- With the help of Right to Information Act and Social Audit they brought the wrong doings in NREGA and other developmental schemes under Manika Block to light. This led to the legal action taken against many Government Staff, Officials and Middlemen.
- On 16th October 2010, the Maoists organised a Kangaroo court (Jan Adalat) and locked down the houses of Neyamat and Bhukhan Singh. Maoists accused them of embezzlement, felling forest trees and collecting money in the name of providing ownership rights of the forest land. Next day police removed the locks. In the evening the Maoists came and put the house under locks again. After this incident PUCL General Secretary Shashibhushan Pathak and four members of PUC1 Palamau, reached there and formed a peace committee. Five members from both the sides constituted this committee. This committee was given the responsibility to put an end to this conflict. Peace committee has already met twice over this matter and third meeting was scheduled on March 13th 2011.

But prior to this meeting on 2ndMarch itself, Neyamat Ansari was killed.

- He clearly said that a nexus between local middlemen, Govt. officials and Maoists is responsible of this incident (Murder).
- He said Maoists have made baseless allegations against him. The Investigation Team of PUCL has verified it from the villagers and found it to be baseless.

In order to get to the depth of the incidence and to strive for justice for the victims, the Fact Finding Team made a visit to the Jeroowa village, Panchayat Kope, Block Manika, District Latehar, on 18th March 2011.

"Manika is situated 160 Kms west of state capital Ranchi. It falls under Latehar District and is a Block headquarters too. One of the revenue villages of kope panchayat, Jeroowa Village is about 4 kms away from Manika Block Headquarters. Both the houses of Neyamat Ansari and Bhukhan Singh is situated at Baiga hamlet (tola) the distance between these two houses is one km."

Niyamat Ansari used to live in a joint family. The house contained 4 rooms with tiled roof over 5 decimal of land. The rooms were horizontally divided using woods and bamboo. The family had inherent property of 0.09 acres of land and 2 acres had been gifted at the Bhu Daan period. Among the source of income were the agricultural land and daily vages. The agricultural production had not led to good income the year. Elder brother Hadees though had 'Red Card' but no rice or wheat was being given to him through this card. All the three brothers of the family had MNREGA job cards but lack of regular employment forced them to migrate outside the state.

According to the villagers, Niyamat Ansari had been killed because he was making efforts for proper implementation of MNREGA scheme. He was a social activist and was associated with 'Gram Swaraj' organisation. He was creating awareness about various schemes including MNREGA and National Forest Rights Act among the villagers. This led to a tiff between him and the local contractors -middlemen & the forest mafia. Neyamat's Sister Mosmat Shahida Bibi told that during the construction of check dam Neyamat was manhandled and beaten up because he advocated for minimum wages be paid to the labourers.

Arun Singh, Shankar Dubey and Vijay Tiwary threatened him of dire consequences. Jitan Singh and Jokhan Singh of Jeroowa village agreed that this incident was true.

Arun Singh threatened Neyamat's elder brother Hadees Miyan "reason with your brother or else he will meet the same fate as Lalit Mehta." The above mentioned contractors came around four times to his house before his killing to threaten him. During the Social Audit a pond was constructed in Bandarchoowan, Rankikala. Shanker Dubey was its Contractor, he told Neyamat Ansari "you don't have any rights to speak to the Social Audit, So you are not supposed to say anything." Neyamat Anwari's Jeroowa village was selected for construction of a pond, but it was shifted somewhere else by the contractors. This too ensured a fight between Neyamat Ansari and the Middlemen.

Following is the detailed description of the incidence as recorded by the team-

A Brahmin family of village Kope, supported by a contractor called the Maoists and held a meeting on Bhootgarhwa ground in the outskirts of the village, close to the forest. This meeting between Maoists and the Brahmin family was held in the month of October 2010. After this meeting only the Maoists came to village Jeroowa and locked down the houses of Neyamat Ansari and Bhukhan Singh. It happened on 23rd October 2010. On 24 Oct 2010 the next day police came around 3.00 pm and broke open the locks. The same night militants came and locked the door again and his elder brother and sister were beaten up.

In a meeting after four days mediated by Manika Police it was agreed that Neyamat's old mother can stay in the house after breaking the locks open. Nearly after four months the Maoists visited again. Around 7.30 pm they took Neyamat to the outskirts of the village and began thrashing him. The militants were around 15-16 in number, armed with guns. When they were thrashing him up, Neyamat's sister went there to protect him but she was threatened on gunpoint to back off or else will be shot. Then she sat there on the ground and started crying. Neyamat was beaten up with sticks not less than hundred times. When he was half dead Maoists told a village woman to go and tell his family that they can take Neyamat where ever they wish. He was carried over the shoulders and brought home from the place of the incident. Immediately he was put on a cot and was carried to Manika Hospital. There the doctors referred him to Latehar for better treatment. He was brought to Latehar Hospital from Manika in an ambulance by the Administration, where he died after 10 minutes. Neyamat's father tried to gather the villagers, he went to their homes but fear stricken villagers were not willing to help. Bhukhan Singh's brother Jokhan Singh told "we were busy with the construction work of a NREGA Pond since morning, the day Neyamat was killed. While returning in evening we saw two kids, aged around 13-14 years, one was Bhukhan's son the other was Sukar's grandson. Both the kids are studying in 7th-8th Standard, members of the squad got hold of them and took them to their old home. It was locked. When the mothers of both the kids reached there and started crying then only the kids were released. Neyamat Ansari was killed in front of Birbal Singh, Basudev Singh and Pehalwan Singh."

The government machineries were found to give a lukewarm response towards the incidence and killin of Niyamat Ansari. The road was blocked with the dead body. The Latehar DC gave an assurance of government assistance. A request by the villagers was made in written for compensation of Rs 10 lakhs, a house, pension and job to the dependent. But what really was provided was only pension of Rs 10,000. Morover, the police camp was set up in the Kope village, where the murderers lived, instead of providing security to the villagers. The family was threatened by the police to take back the case. No police, administration or any government machineiy had ever visited the place for vigilance of the security measures. All this indicated the fact that instead of the victims, the culprits were being protected. According to Niyamat's sister who had filed the FIR, eight persons were alleged but nothing concrete was being done in this regard. 30 to 36 houses of the forest land of the Kope village had been burnt, and FIR had been made against 26 villagers. The movement to get the leasehold of forest land was on.

Niyamat Ansari was alleged of collecting four to five thousand per person in lieu of getting the lease of the forest land and also for cutting and selling the forest threes. He was said to be a police informer. But all the villagers, including the Head of "Gram Sabha" Madhyam Singh S/o Tani Singh rubbished these allegations and told that due to the movement started by Neyamat, they were able to get respect and minimum wages. The Ration Dealer was made to deliver the full quota of grains/ration. It was the forest officials who sell timber on the sly.

The team found that FIR had been filed against innocent people, no teak tree existed in the area, but the charges against them were of felling the trees. Niyamat and Bhukhan Singh were imprisoned for this and many had warrants against themselves. The Maoists party was silent on the matter of burning of houses. According to Jokhan Singh and Jeetan Singh of Bahrai Tola (hamlet), the allegations made against Niyamat were a punishment to him to create awareness of NREGA, not in the matter of forest land. Niyamat Ansari was killed the very next day of the filing of case against the BDO and Panchayat Sewak.

The following conclusion was made by the investigation team:-

- Neyamat Ansari was murdered to serve the selfish ulterior motives of the Govt. officials & staff, local contractors and Maoists.
- The allegations made by Maoists against Neyamat Ansari and Bhubhan Singh were found baseless.
- The actions taken by the police right after the incident arouse suspicion because they were camping in village kope, which is one km. away from jeroowa, the village of victim's families. It was all done in the name of giving protection to victim's families. Furthermore the contractors and middlemen involved in this murder case lived in kope village.
- The organisations Neyamat Ansari and Bhubhan Singh worked for didn't make any arrangements for their security while working in field. Whereas they were facing open threats in carrying out a risky job. Their social security was ignored as well. It was found during investigation that the honorarium Neyamat and Bhukhan received against their work was stopped four months prior to this incident.
- Close associate of Neyamat Ansari, Bhukhan Singh faces threat to his life, but any significant act from the organisation is still awaited.

After the incident families of Neyamat Ansari and Bhukhan Singh were frightened and went through severe financial crisis. Also the people of Jeroowa and nearby villages were left to live in terror. Neyamat Ansari and Bhukhan Singh had fought for social justice, people's right and laborer's right. They also raised their voice against corruption and made sure that people get their rights.

(*Source:* INVESTIGATION TEAM'S REPORT on Neyamat Ansari murder case Manika [Jharkhand])

Analytical. Perspectives

The financial incentives to the naxal groups are offered by their muscle power, their enormous presence at grassroot levels, and such collusive arrangements with politicians, government officials and contractors. Morover, the state often is not able to enforce its writs in the naxal affected areas. These extremists impose levy on government projects. Such collections ranges from forest contractors, civil contractors, businessmen, government officials(police in some areas), villagers. "The Naxalites have also threatened the Golden Quadrilateral project in their areas of influence. As a result, progress in these areas is probably the slowest of the GQ stretches. In fact, the Naxal fear is not restricted to this area or to the PM highway alone. They have also threatened companies such as Steel Authority of India Limited-run iron ore mines at Megahahatburu." Unlike their false claims of ideological wards, these Naxal groups now are indulged in money making. Smuggling of woods, taking cut from government officials from development fund and extortion have become main business of Naxalites. Stories of deviations and degenerations have become common phenomena in the media. The dwindled ideological perspectives and financial incentives have led to criminalisation of the groups. Often the local commanders in lack of ideological indoctrination and lure of money are found to behave like ordinary criminals. Degeneration in Naxalite movement resulted in emergence of protection racket. Even joining the movement has become a source for safety from law for some with criminal background. Lack of state response and failure of administrative machineries at grassroots level has been the main reason for sustenance of the menace of Naxalism. Many state officials do not even attend their offices due to the threat and fear of Naxal violent attacks due to this which further leads to lack of development.

Lack of adequate police services has also been among the causes- lack of attempt to equip police forces properly.

Despite of the fact that the Jharkhand government heavily relied on police services to neutralize the armed groups, The police operations suffer due to lack of adequate and appropriate equipment - including basics such as automatic weapons, landmine detectors, transport and communications; a proper intelligence network at the grassroots level; and better protection to police officers and personnel in the Naxalite affected areas. Despite of the mass arrests under the POTA, the government was unable to restrain the violence.

The surrender policies of the government have also not been fruitful. The reason for this apart from its weak implementation mechanisms, are the ruthless Naxal retaliation measures towards the deserters. Maoists have been ruthless in dealing with the deserters and any activist who felt tempted by the surrender package must be ready to face the consequences.

Yet another reason has been the failure of the government in proper implementation of the land reform policies. The village economy still supports nearly three fourth of the population, but remains among the most exploitative. The poor implementation has also been consequences of the political influences of the land owning classes, "the factors that sustained the movement and pattern of politics remains the same in these States and if the forces that shaped the course of the Naxalite movement remain in the control of socio-political and administrative structures of these States, and Naxalites do not make any positive intervention to alter them, the recent trends in ideological synergy and resultant upsurge in violence cannot be interpreted as any fundamental change in the character of Naxalite groups."

(*Source:* www.asthabharati.org/Dia AprQ5/Sanj.htm)

According to the members of the district administration,, lack of proper governance is the cause for such intense terror by the Maoists. Last time when the polls took place in Jharkhand, a candidate who got elected was in jail on charges of allegedly being a Naxal commander in several districts. Such is the Naxal influence on the political circumference. Those political leaders, not having links that act as hurdle in countering naxalism, unfortunately don't posses the will for countering. There are reports that the police/CRPF have on some occasion surrounded major Naxal meetings with their top commanders attending it, but have failed to yield any result. Either they have failed to strike on time, or even if they have, they have been unable to get desired results. This is enough to suggest an intelligence failure, or it tells us that the intelligence of the Naxals is better timed, if not more efficient, than that of the system. Often the Naxals have hit hard, but the administration has failed to hit back and carry on combing operations of the required level.

(*Source:* zeenews.india.com/.../lest-we-forget-jharkhand-another-naxal-hotbed_63...)

Naxalism in Jharkhand has also been influential during the electoral processes. "Naxalite Movement in Bihar and Jharkhand" mentions an estimate of such influences in 54 out of 81 constituencies till the respective time period (till 2005). Supports to political parties at the time of elections grant them favorable context for operation after elections. The surprising consequence had been noted when despite of violence and pole boycotts there was no noticeable decline in vote percentage. For example, during the April 2004 Parliamentary Election in Jharkhand, where the pre-poll campaign was marred by a series of attacks on security force personnel, the voter turnout was recorded at 55.71 percent. Even in some of the worst-affected districts, including Palamu, Hazaribagh, Singhbhum and Lohardaga, the voter turnout ranged between 49 and 60 per cent.

(*Source:* www.asthabharati.orR/Dia Apr05/Sanj.htm)

Recorded data included in the article "Naxalism in Jharkhand shows the increase in naxal insurgencies at the time of each election, and had crossed all limits till 2009. Despite of this, the population still has faith on the democratic politics and increase in number of voters had also been noted.

Jharkhand since its inception has been known for its unstable government. It has been a hot bed for Naxals. Districts of Palamu, Chatra, Latehar, Gumla, lohardagga are Naxal affected districts. Other than these, 12 other districts are also prone to the Naxal menace and have been converted to safe zones by Maoists for themselves. The counter activities such as operations by the police and Para military forces have not deterred the spread of Naxalism in the state. The reasons have been lack of political will and connections of big political leaders cutting across the party lines with the Maoists.

A unique feature of the capital of Jharkhand, Ranchi is that it is surrounded by three army cantonment which provides good cover to the capital. This is the reason for lack of any major Naxal or terror attack in the state capital. But the stories of Naxal land mine blasts and firings are prominent in the outskirts of Ranchi. This in a manner poses a threat to the state capital of Naxals spreading their wings inside, "the paramilitary and state police and anti-Naxal forces are in constant threat of being attacked by the extremists. Their vehicles ply on the roads and highways under the threat of a landmine blast or gun attack by the Maoists."

(*Source:* "zeenews.india.com/.../lest-we-forget-jharkhand-another-naxal-hotbed_63../' and "Naxallism in Jharkhand")

'हिंसा नहीं है किसी भी समस्या का हल'

K.K

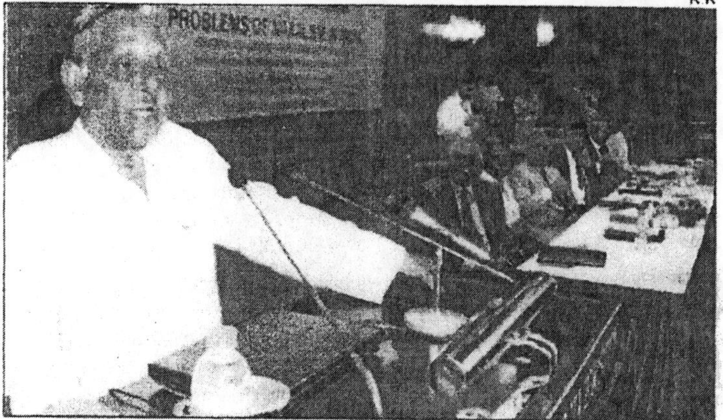

एमिटी यूनिवर्सिटी में गुरुवार को करगिल विजय दिवस के मौके पर आयोजित एक सेमिनार में शामिल हुए पूर्व केंद्र मंत्री मणिशंकर अय्यर

एस ॥ नोएडा : नक्सलवाद की समस्या को लेकर युनाइटेड सॉल्यूशन ऑफ इंडिया और एमिटी यूनिवर्सिटी में गुरुवार को करगिल विजय दिवस के मौके पर एक सेमिनार का आयोजन किया गया। इस मौके पर पूर्व केंद्र मंत्री और राज्यसभा सांसद मणिशंकर अय्यर चीफ गेस्ट के रूप में मौजूद थे। इस दौरान कई रिटायर्ड आर्मी ऑफिसर ने नक्सलवाद पर अपने विचार रखे। मणिशंकर अय्यर ने सेमिनार में आए लोगों से कहा कि नक्सलवाद को खत्म करने के लिए सबसे पहले हर तबके को जागरूक करना होगा। हिंसा किसी भी समस्या का हल नहीं है, नक्सलियों को मुख्य धारा से जोड़ना जरूरी है। उन्होंने कहा कि नक्सलवाद को जड़ से खत्म करने के लिए एजुकेशन के स्तर में सुधार जरूरी है। इसके लिए हम सबको आगे आने की जरूरत है।

Chapter – IX

Conclusion

The principle behind the Naxal movement was the will to establish the rule of proletariats. With this aim, there began a revolution by the proletariats. This principle of Karl Marx was further followed and executed by Lenin. Mao Zedong interpreted this in the way that he made his followers believe that "Power is followed by the barrel of gun." Thus movements went on in the name of revolutionaries and proletariats with the faith that armed rebellion and violence will lead to power.

The initiatives in India were made by the Telangana struggle just after the independence, but resulted in complete unsuccessfulness due to a lack of solidarity. The real identity was gained by the movement in Naxalbari in West Bengal with the efforts of Cheru Majumdar. This movement then really with great commitment made the poor and deprived participations. Educated and elite classes also were the participants. It gained such momentous that then Siddharth Shankar Ray's government weakened. Attempts were made by the government to crush the movement and thousands were killed and imprisoned. Though this led to a break in the movement, still there were believes of furtherance in the direction on the basis of its principles. The activities further included formation of Peoples' War in Andhra and MCC in Jharkhand.

But these people failed to realize that the legal power of the government and security forces of arms and right to use them were much greater than what relied in their illegal methods. They also failed to realize that the power and fear from illegal arms revolt won't be able to retain the masses with the movement at the time when efforts by the state would be made to crush it. The difference between Gandhi's ideology and that of Maoism lies here- Mahatma Gandhi arose the moral aspirations of people towards revolution and then brought the change unlike the naxalites. the Naxal crusaders failed in retaining a mental power in this sense. The greatest disadvantage which the people in affected area face is the threats of the armed force of the police, state and authority on one hand; and of the Naxalites on the other. Naxalism prevails in the states of Chattisgarh, Bihar and Jharkhand. The state of Jharkhand since last two years has become the most vulnerable with the highest number of nasal incidences in the state. This has been a consequence of the failure of legal and governmental machineries. Inegalitarian situations had made people join the Naxal groups an they saw Maoism as the only solution to overcome inequality. But the situation today is that Naxalism has evolved as the greatest barrier in smooth development of areas, all these advancing to form a vicious cycle. When the sources to acquire justice, and to have development were curbed by corrupt means, and inhabitation of naxal forces increased in these areas, the political forces escaped mostly from during the period of globalisation in 1990s and consequent changes which overthrew much of the older systems. In the period when Bihar with the territory of today's Jharkhand was under the chiefministership of Lalu Yadav, and Madhya Pradesh with today's Chattisgarh under that of Digvijay Singh, these uprisings were not given much importance and the issue remained a neglected one. This resulted in such disadvantage that Naxalism became accepted phenomena, though between the arms of state authorities and Naxalites, the people supported no one. But to those classes that had suffered tortures such as rape, unchastity, arbitrary land acquisition seeked for hopes with the Naxal groups to have justice which can be termed forceful.

The thing to be remembered and coined here is that power of arms and violence can never be sustainable and does not *give* room for analytical diplomacies. The group and its leaders particularly applied all those strategies and ways in the name of the proletariats, what the ruling and exploitative classes had been applying earlier. So, such a set up obviously cannot have human being at its core value, but arms. Such a system where no human view but only a superior exploitative power has importance can never help to gain success in achieving an egalitarian society.

Later, the Naxal groups went on weakening and splitting due to several reasons. Levy extraction has remained to be the main aim of these groups now and has been quite easy for them. The leader of maoist squads often are non tribals. Groups originated from the main stream such as the Tritiya Prastuti Committee (TPC), at the same time counter organisations such as the Salvajudum had been organised by the governments.

The Naxals have made an elusive picture of indulgence in a fight against the corporate sectors. The corporate very cleverly are smoothening their works by lending levies. The naxals from this are also being benefited in the manner that they are able to make huge money for powerful weapons to counter their enemies. Splits within many of the naxal groups have occurred, the cadres from which have also joined the police to help counter the maoist squads. The corporate have done the same with naxal groups what they did with the political system- have added up to the corrupt ideologies. The model for development in India is not an indigenous one but has been adopted as an American model with principles of maximum profit and maximum consumption. In such a system, inequality can very easily penetrate. The vulnerable sections then are the first to suffer and get the least. This is unlike the earlier principle of cooperation with nature in such a manner to encourage an egalitarian system; one would work according to one's capacity and would get according to one's ability and merit. The Indian corporate system in this manner inherits the corruption and violence. The Adivasi population mostly resides in the forests and mineral rich areas. A corporate ideology certainly has a mentality of evacuating people from such areas which with maximum efforts of resettlement and compensations, still cannot anyhow equate and satisfy livelihood.

Towards a Solution

The three pronged solution of: Social and economic development, multilateral dialogue and military force-need to be focused. In coming up with strategies for national economic growth, the government must always bear in mind the possible effects of fast growth for all socio-economic groups in a country as large and diverse as India.

Former President APJ Abdul Kalam on views on Naxalism, highlighted on the fact that Maoism is prevalent in the areas where land reforms had not been successful. He stressed on to bring inclusive land reforms in these areas. Another thing that he emphasized is lending of earning capacity to every person. People also become part of naxal cadres, after being frustrated from unemployment and inaccessibleness to profitable income. PURA (Providing Urban Amenities in Rural Areas) according to him can be of great help. Employment programs ought to be made free from their unwanted drawbacks.

It is not that the above cannot be achieved from a domestic model of production.

In an inegaliterian society, aggressiveness is certain to follow. However, the outcome can be in three forms- a verbal abuse, physical assault, or the third is to remove the causes of such aggressiveness toward others. This third method is what Mahatma Gandhi promoted. Gandhi's path,

"Gandhiwad" is a sustainable and long lasting solution. The Supreme Court for the first time applied the Forest Rights Act in April 2013, in a president setting decision. It gave the right to the local communities to decide over the matter of further carrying on of a project in the area through public meetings and voting. Vedanta Ltd had plans to mine bauxite at the top on the Niyamgiri Hill for processing in the nearby large Lanjigarh factory. The victory strengthens the hope for tribal safety and undisturbed settlements over violent struggles.

"Violence cannot be ended through violence." Rights of each should be made available. Also among the solutions, monopoly of the corporate houses should be put to limits. Washing out of the menace of Naxalism is impossible even for military efforts or for any government without it. The most dangerous aspect of growing Naxal insurgencies is that often innocent people are convicted by police as Maoists. The counter naxal trends themselves have been causes of human rights violation. Those who are fighting through peaceful weapons of Gandhi, Lohia, and Jai Prakash Narayan, if convicted of being indulged in terrorist activities, the door to solutions would be shut down. Supreme Court in its "Samta Judgement" had declared to pay shares to the dalit or adivasi whose land is being encroached so that he or she also gets share in the benefit acquired from the land. The prevailing law only provides compensation in return. For proper functioning of the whole system, each and every part should be in a good working position. Likewise, the fruits of development should be fully made to the people, efficacy in the implementation is a must to tackle all such problems.

Only 10 to 15 per cent of the total amount for development if really is invested for implementation of measures, this certainly is a matter of worry. A government's direct cash transfer program leverages Aadhar numbers and banking networks across the country for transfer cash subsidies directly to the beneficiaries of government welfare schemes. Despite, the corruption hights are big hurdles. The villages should be blended with autonomous authority. Development in these villages should be made on the basis of the resources available there indigenously; markets should be put to flourishment, and least of foreign goods and services should be encouraged. Through these steps, the greed among people and entrepreneur groups will lessen down. This greed is that which makes such corporate encroach more and more land and evacuate more and more people from settlements. Need is to enhance systems in such a manner, that necessities are made available to people to their doors. The political parties which in the name of the poor and downtrodden stand in elections, should come forward to really work for these people through systems such as decentralisation.

Naxalism, is an outcome of the present system. Until and unless changes for good are not brought in the administrative and social systems, Naxalism cannot be eradicated.

References

"Naxalwad, Sawalon Ke Katghare Mein" by- Prasann Kumar Choudhary

"Naxalism in Jharkhand" by IPS (Retd.) Bimal Kishore Sinha

"Strategic intervention for Accelerating Development in Jharkhand[1] Editors- Dr.(Mrs) Pushpa Mandal and Dr Umesh Kumar Verma (Published in 2000).

PRWC: Introduction to Indian society and revolution, Ang Bayan, 19 July 2013 - philippinerevolution.

"Jharkhand records highest Naxal violence this year" -Times Of India articles.timesofindia.indiatimes.com >

"Maoist: Jharkhand Assessment 2013 - South Asia Terrorism Portal" www.satp.org/satporgtp/countries/india/.../Assessment/.../Jharkhand.htm

About Jharkhand | UNDP

www.undp.org/content/india/en/home/.. Jharkhand/about-Jharkhand en.wikipedia.org/wiki/Jharkhand

www.traveljharkhand.com/iharkhand-tourism/districts-in-iharkhand.html

Marginal fall in tribal population in Jharkhand - Times Of India articles.timesofindia.indiatimes.com www.asthabharati.org/Dia Apr05/Sani.htm

Corporate and the Maoists nexus - Asian Centre for Human Rights www.achrweb.org/ihrrq/issuel/coq3orate.html "The tribal cause is a mask to further the Naxal agenda strategicstudyindia.blogspot.com/..ythe-trjbal-causeHSmask-t-..)o-further.ht Analysis of the situation in 2012 | Naxalite Maoist India naxalrevolution.blogspot.com/2012/04/analysis-of-situation-in-2012.html

Fact Finding Team's Report on the Massacre in Baruhatu Village Under Bundu Block (Birsa, Ngo)

Report of an investigative study made by the **Anti operation green hunt Citizen's Forum (BIRSA, NGO)**

INVESTIGATION TEAM'S REPORT on Neyamat Ansari murder case Manika [Jharkhand] (BIRSA, NGO)

zeenews.india.com/.../lest-we-forget-jharkhand-another-naxal-hotbed_63...

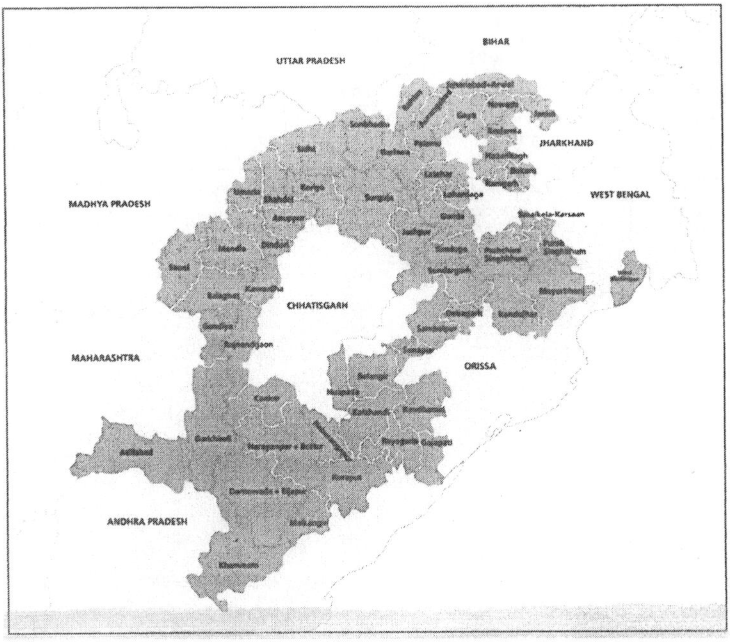

Map showing the first 60 IAP districts. The Ring of Fire in Central India is now spread across 78 districts in 9 states.

The Ring of Fire

Operation green hunt will be focussed on 78 IAP districts spread across 9 states identified by the GOl. These districts form a ring in central India and are the most affected by Maoist Insurgency. OGH aims to clear these areas of Maoists and then launch so called developmental activities.

Deaths related to violence

Period	*Civilians*	*Security forces*	*Insurgents*	*Total per period*
1989-2001	1,610	432	1,007	3,049
2002	382	100	141	623
2003	410	105	216	731
2004	466	100	87	653
2005	524	153	225	902
2006	521	157	274	952
2007	460	236	141	837
2008	399	221	214	834
2009	586	317	217	1,120
2010	713	285	171	1,169
2011	275	128	199	602
2012	146	104	117	367
2013	123	83	136	342
TOTAL	**6,615**	**2,421**	**3,145**	**12,181**

Reds continue poster war in Giridih villages

Dhanbad: The CPI(Maoist) continued with its poster war against panchayati raj in the rural pockets of Pirtand and Dumri blocks of Giridih district despite the state police launching anti-Maoist operations in many districts.

Three Maoist-hit blocks of the district, including Pirtand, Dumri and Bago-dar will vote in the fourth and last phase of the panchayat election on December 12.

Apart from protesting against the ongoing anti- Maoist operations, Maoists have asked villagers to stay away from polling. A number of posters and pamphlets were seen in the remote villages of Pirtand and Dumri blocks in the past week.

Giridih SP Kuldeep Dwi-vedi said elaborate security arrangements have been made to ensure peaceful election. "We have so far been successful in our strategy to contain Left extremism during the last three phases of the rural polls. The state police, along with CRPF, are working together to prevent any untoward incidents," Dwivedi added.

"Even if the rebels stick posters or distribute pamphlets, it would not deter people from casting their votes. A majority of villagers, sections of which were earlier considered as Maoist sympathizers, are either contesting elections or supporting their neighbours or kin", said Irden Ekka, commandant of the Parasnath-based 154 battalion of the CRPE

A total of 224 polling stations, of a total of 987 in all three blocks, including 87 in Dumri, 75 in Pirtand and 62 in Bagodar blocks of the district, have been declared hypersensitive.

आदिवासियों को सशक्त बनाए जाने की जरूरत : अय्यर

नेशनल दुनिया संवाददाता

नोएडा। हमें आदिवासीयों के मन को समझने की आवश्यकता है जो बार-बार स्वयं को विस्थापित पाते है। जब तक सरकार इन आदिवासियों को सशक्त नही बनाएगी तब तक नक्सल समस्या को सुलझाना मुश्किल है। ये बातें राज्यसभा सांसद मणिशंकर अय्यर ने गुरुवार को यहां कहीं। वह एमिटी विवि में 'भारत में नक्सल समस्या सुलझाने के क्षेत्र मे जमीनी वास्तविकता एवं चुनौतियां' विषय पर आयोजित परिचर्चा को संबोधित कर रहे थे।

उन्होंने कहा कि आदिवासी लंबे समय से वन मे रहते आए हैं। उनका सारा जीवन वनों के ईद-गिर्द ही रहा है। जिनकी आर्थिक जीवन शैली का स्तर भी निम्न रहा है उनमें निराशा, क्रोध, बढ़ा है। उन्होंने कहा कि आजादी के उपरांत आधुनिकता का उत्थान हुआ उसके उपरांत

छात्रों को संबोधित करते राज्यसभा के सदस्य मणिशंकर अय्यर।

करीब 60 से 65 मिलियन आदिवासियों का विस्थापन हुआ। आर्थिक विकास की मांग रहती है कि ज्यादातर संसाधनों का धरती से दोहन हो जिससे जीडीपी की वृद्धि हो लेकिन हम वहां के लोगों के बारे मे ध्यान नहीं देते जिनकी जीविका उन्हीं संसाधनों के बल पर चलती है।

श्री अय्यर ने कहा कि अगर देश के आर्थिक विकास में वृद्धि हो रही है तो वही दूसरी ओर कुछ लोगों का मुख्यधारा से अलगाव भी बढ़ा है। उन्होंने कहा कि हाल के वर्षो मे आदिवासी संपदा पर बाहरी लोगों का अधिपत्य कायम हो गया है। क्योंकि ज्यादात्तर खनिज संसाधन उसी भूमि पर पाये जाते है जहां पर आदिवासी सदियां से रह रहे हैं। उन्होंने गृह मंत्रालय की रिपोर्ट का जिक्र करते हुए कहा कि तीन जिलों में एक जिला या तो आंशिक रूप से या पृथक रूप से वांमपथी उग्रवाद से ग्रस्त है।

250 सैन्य अधिकारियों ने भी लिया हिस्सा

यूनाइटेड सर्विस इंस्टीट्यूशन ऑफ इंडिया एवं एमिटी विवि के संयुक्त तत्वावधान में आयोजित परिचर्चा में 250 सैन्य अधिकारियों ने भी हिस्सा लिया। जिनमें कई वर्तमान में कार्यरत भी हैं जबकि कई अधिकारी सेवानिवृत्त हो चुके हैं। इनमें मुख्य रूप से त्रिपुरा व छत्तीसगढ़ के पूर्व राज्यपाल लेफ्टिनेंट जनरल के.एम. सेठ, लेफ्ट. जनरल वी.के. अहलुवालिया, पूर्व आर्मी कमांडर, सेंट्रल कमांड, ई.एन. राममोहन सहित कई अन्य अधिकारी शामिल थे।

INDEX

P

R

S